# Essential Elements of

# Marketing

## Roderick Smith

Roderick Smith is a Senior Consultant with Cast Metals Development Ltd, a company providing technical and marketing services to the foundry industry. He also teaches evening classes in marketing at South Birmingham College to those studying for the various Chartered Institute of Marketing examinations.

*Series adviser:* Bob Cudmore BEd, MBA, Head of Management and Professional Studies Division, South Birmingham College

*Technical adviser:* Margaret O'Gorman BA Econ (Hons), PGCE, South Birmingham College

Published in association with South Birmingham College
DP Publications Ltd
1995

SOUTH
BIRMINGHAM
COLLEGE

## Acknowledgments

This book is dedicated to my wife Mary and to my children Duncan, James and Rebecca, who make it all worthwhile.

Thanks also to Paul Stallard, for having shown me that there is more to marketing than I had once thought, to Bob Cudmore, for the opportunity to teach, and to Margaret O'Gorman, for her comments on the first draft of this book.

A CIP catalogue reference for this book is available from the British Library

ISBN  1 85805 102 9

Typeset by Elizabeth Elwin, London

Printed in Great Britain by the Guernsey Press Co. Ltd, Vale, Guernsey

# Preface

## Aim

The aim of the *Essential Elements* series is to provide course support material covering the main subject areas of HND/C Business Studies and equivalent level courses at a price that students can afford. Students can select titles to suit the requirements of their own particular courses whether BTEC Certificate in Business Administration, Certificate in Marketing, IPS Foundation, Institute of Bankers, Access to Business Studies, Institute of Personnel Management, or other appropriate undergraduate and professional courses.

Many courses now have a modular structure, i.e. individual subjects are taught in a relatively short period of, say, 10 to 12 weeks. The *Essential Elements* series meets the need for material which can be built into the students' study programmes and used for directed self-study. All the texts, therefore, include activities with answers for students' self-assessment, activities for lecturer-assessment, and references to further reading.

The series is a joint venture between DP Publications and South Birmingham College.

## How to use the series

All the books in the series are intended to be used as workbooks and provide approximately 70 hours of study material. Each text covers the essential elements of that subject, so that the core of any course at this level is covered, leaving the lecturer to add supplementary material if required. All have the following features:

☐ **In-text activities,** which aim to promote understanding of the principles, and are set at frequent intervals in the text. The solutions add to the student's knowledge, as well as providing an introduction to the next learning point.

☐ **End of chapter exercises**, some of which are intended for self-assessment by the student (these have solutions at the back of the book). Others are suitable for setting by the lecturer and answers or marking guides are provided in the Lecturers' Supplement. These exercises include progress and review questions, multiple choice questions, which test specific knowledge and allow rapid marking, practice questions, questions for advanced students, and assignments.

☐ **Further reading references** for students who wish to follow up particular topics in more depth.

☐ **Lecturers' Supplement**, which is available free of charge to lecturers adopting the book as a course text. It includes answers or guides to marking to help with student assessment.

## Other titles in the series

Available now: Business Economics, Business Statistics, Quantitative Methods, Management Accounting, Financial Accounting.

Available 1995: Human Resource Management, Business Information Systems.

Available 1996: Business Law, Total Quality Management.

# Contents

## 3  Promotion

## 4  Selling as part of marketing

## 5 Pricing policy

## 6 Place and Distribution

## 7 Marketing Research

## 8 Marketing management

## Appendix

## Index

# 1 Survey methods

## 1.1 Introduction

Ask people within any business what they understand by the term marketing and what a marketing department does and you will get a variety of answers:

"it's all about advertising"

"the people who put our brochures together"

"it is the company's sales activities".

Although some of these answers encompass something of what marketing is about, they by no means answer the question "what is marketing".

This first chapter of *The Essential Elements of Marketing* will provide an elementary answer to the question of what marketing is all about. Later chapters in the book will look more closely at specific aspects of marketing.

At the end of this chapter the student should

❏ be able to define what marketing is, and understand what the definition means

❏ know what is meant by the marketing mix

❏ understand how and why macro environmental factors must be considered

❏ know the different ways in which a company can organise its marketing operations.

### Activity 1

What do you understand by the term marketing? Write down your definition, and then see how it compares with your understanding when you have finished the course associated with this book.

## 1.2 A definition of marketing

Many writers and practitioners of marketing have attempted to define it. However, probably the best modern definition is that put forward by the Chartered Institute of Marketing (CIM):

"Marketing is the management process which identifies, anticipates and supplies customer requirements efficiently and profitably."

To understand this definition fully, we need to look at it in more detail.

First, marketing is a management process. This means that it is a planned activity within the whole of the company's operations. It is not something that just happens, an ad hoc activity. As a management process it will be budgeted and expected to plan its activities and show results.

The second part of this definition talks of identifying, anticipating and supplying customer requirements. This should be the absolute aim of all businesses, and all those involved in any sort of business. Customer requirements are the reason we go to work each day. If we are not interested in fulfilling customer requirements, then there is no point in being in business. Marketing is about identifying what these requirements are; it helps to anticipate what they might be in the future and ensures that the product or service that is supplied will meet the customer's requirements.

Finally, this definition says that the customer requirements must be met in a way that is efficient and thus profitable. Efficiency will ensure that resources are not wasted, whether they are material or human resources. As for profitability, a company that is not profitable will not stay in business for long. If you have a product that fulfils customer requirements, then the customers will pay for it. What the supplier has to do is set a price that allows the company to make a profit yet meets the customer's expectation for the price of the product.

Thus marketing is focused on customers, and is a set of management techniques for fulfilling those customers' requirements in a way that allows the company to make a profit and so stay in business.

## Activity 2

List some companies which you believe apply marketing effectively, and some which do not.

In the above lists you may have identified companies such as Marks & Spencer, Kodak, Apple Computers, Proctor & Gamble, Dulux Paints, McDonalds or Ford as being good at marketing. Conversely, companies with a poor marketing performance might include British Rail (simply calling passengers 'customers' does not produce a customer-driven approach to business).

Before going further, it is worth looking at two other approaches that companies may adopt. The first of these is called a 'sales' orientation. In this approach, the whole emphasis of the company is on selling. A product is made and then a well-trained and highly motivated salesforce (probably being paid commission only) goes out to sell it. These companies rely heavily on promotional methods to sell the product, often involving what is termed a 'hard sell'.

Some examples of sales-oriented companies would include double-glazing companies, insurance companies, and certain industrial commodities (for example, cleansing agents). It should be noted, however, that not all double-glazing, insurance and industrial commodities companies fall into this category, and many do adapt a more acceptable customer-oriented, marketing approach to business. The important point to note is that a sales-oriented company is more interested in selling the product that in the needs of the person buying it.

The second type of company is product or production oriented. These tend to be companies that are good at producing certain products or types of products, and go on producing them even when sales decline and some elementary market research would tell them that customers want something different. A typical and oft-quoted example of a product-oriented company is the British motorcycle industry, which may have made superb motorcycles but was destroyed by the Japanese manufacturers because they made what people wanted and needed.

By contrast to the above two scenarios, a marketing-oriented company takes as its starting point the market in which it operates and thus the needs of its customers. It is by satisfying these needs that the company will make a profit and so stay in business.

---

### Activity 3

List some examples of sales-oriented and production-oriented companies.

---

## 1.3 The marketing mix

The marketing mix is the term used for the four marketing variables, or the four elements of marketing over which the company can exercise control.

They are

PRODUCT

PROMOTION

PRICE

PLACE

and are also referred to as 'the Four Ps'.

As will become evident in later chapters of this book, the 4 Ps are controllable by the company, i.e. the product can be changed, the promotional methods can be changed, the price can be changed and the placement method can be changed.

Although each element of the marketing mix is dealt with in more detail in later chapters, it is worth briefly discussing them here in the introductory chapter.

### 1.3.1 Product

A product is usually taken to be something real and tangible. When considering a product we should think of the features of the product, its physical appearance, the quality of it, how it is packaged, and most of all the benefits the product brings to the consumer. The idea of benefits is explored more fully in the next chapter.

This idea of features and benefits is very important, as what the consumer really buys is the benefit and it is up to the second P, PROMOTION, to ensure that the consumer is aware of the benefits.

### 1.3.2 Promotion

In this book, promotion is taken to mean advertising, sales promotion, public relations and personal selling.

These are used for a variety of purposes, including telling consumers about a product, explaining the benefits of the product, persuading consumers to try a product, communicating with a company's 'publics' (e.g. shareholders, workers, suppliers), and selling to retail outlets and other members of the distribution chain.

All promotional activities need to be planned, and have objectives which should be achieved within a given time scale.

## Activity 4

What promotional activities does your company or college undertake, and what do you believe to be the purpose of them.

Using the purposes of advertising listed above, give some examples of when each is used (for example, telling consumers about a product through advertising when a new product is launched.

### 1.3.3 Price

A company's pricing policies will encompass more than just the prices asked for its products. It will include credit terms for distributors and retailers, what discounts are available, how and in response to what prices are charged.

Marketing-oriented companies will set prices based on what the market will bear. This depends on consumers' perception of the product (high or low quality and whether it is 'value for money'), the level of supply and demand, the activities of competitors, and the company's strategic objectives.

## Activity 5

How does your company or college set the price for its products? Is this based on marketing or other criteria?

List some products that vary in price depending on where they are bought (e.g. milk bought from a supermarket or a late-night convenience store will be different prices), and explain why there is a price variation. Other products are the same price wherever they are bought (e.g. a first class stamp). Why is this?

### 1.3.4 Place

Place is a shorthand term for methods of distribution and the activities allied to this and also the physical place where the products are purchased.

Distribution is the method by which goods get from the producer to the customer, and obviously the channels of distribution must work efficiently and be in the best interests of all members of a 'channel' of distribution.

## Activity 6

How do the products of a company of your choice reach their customers?

### 1.3.5 Integration of the marketing mix

It is absolutely essential that all four elements of the marketing mix work together. There are many examples of a company undertaking a major promotional campaign, only to find that it does not have enough products in the shops to satisfy the demand it creates, owing to problems with distribution. Also, if a product has a low price, but the advertising suggests that the price should be high owing to the perceptions created in the minds of those seeing the advertisements, then this causes confusion (dissonance) in the minds of consumers and they will not buy a 'cheap' product that they believe should be expensive (and, of course, vice versa).

The rest of this book is intended to explain the elements of the marketing mix in more detail and show how they can be integrated to make a whole that is very much greater than the sum of the parts.

## 1.4  The macro environment

The next factors of concern to marketers are those found in the macro environment in which the company operates. These are called the environmental factors and are commonly taken to be

> political/legal
>
> economic
>
> social/cultural
>
> technological

From the first letter of each of these four influences, they are known as PEST factors.

Some typical constituents of PEST factors may be as follows:

❑ Political/legal

attitude of the government to free trade

environmental laws

laws relating to advertising

❑ Economic

general state of the economy (e.g. growing, recession)

distribution of wealth in the society

❑ Social/cultural

power of the church or other religious groups

number of magazines/newspapers published

strength of traditional family units

leisure activities available

level of car ownership

❑ Technological

These are often product-specific, but could include:

miniaturisation

increasing use of electronic rather than mechanical controls

Good marketing managers will always consider these factors, for the simple reason that they are acting in and on the markets that are of interest to his/her company.

They become especially important when considering launching new products or entering new markets.

## 1.5 Organisation for marketing

There are essentially three ways in which a company can organise its marketing activities: by function, by product or by market.

### 1.5.1 Organisation by function

This is illustrated in Figure 1.1. The advantages of this method are that the members of each functional team will be experts at their particular discipline, whether it is market research, advertising etc.

*Figure 1.1 Organisation of marketing department by function*

However, this method has the disadvantage that the team members will work on all the company's products within all markets, and so will only have a superficial knowledge of both the products and the markets.

### 1.5.2 Organisation by product

This is probably the most common type of organisation and is illustrated in Figure 1.2.

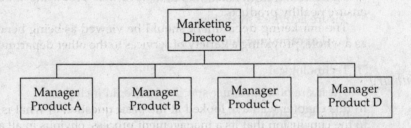

*Figure 1.2 Organisation of marketing department by product*

The product managers will be experts about their particular products, and will be responsible for all marketing activities for that product (or range of products). Thus they will need to know about market research, advertising, distribution, price setting and so on.

The main disadvantage of this set-up is that the product may be sold into several very different markets, and the product manager will therefore need to apply different strategies and tactics in the different markets.

### 1.5.3 Organisation by market

This is illustrated in Figure 1.3 and is a system whereby the market manager is responsible for all the company's products sold into one market. Although the market manager will be hugely knowledgeable about his/her particular market, he may not be so knowledgeable about the products sold into that market, especially if there are a lot of them.

*Figure 1.3 Organisation of marketing department by market*

A further drawback of this system is that different market managers may need very different promotional strategies for one product for different markets.

### Activity 8

How does your company organise its marketing departments? Draw an organisation chart for it.

However the marketing department is organised within a company, it will have to operate within the culture and micro environment of that company. For those companies with a marketing orientation and a belief in staying in business by satisfying customer needs this will be easier than in those companies that rely on selling to keep going or those companies which believe that producing an excellent product will ensure healthy products.

The marketing department should be viewed as being beneficial to the company as a whole, providing a variety of services to the other departments.

## 1.6 Summary

In this chapter we have looked at the basic question of what is marketing, and come to the conclusion that its a management process, obvious in all a company's activities, aimed at satisfying customer requirements.

❏ Marketing activities are based around the 'Marketing Mix' known as the 4 Ps of PRODUCT, PROMOTION, PRICE and PLACE.

❏ However, all marketing takes place within the macro environment, which is subject to a number of influences. These can be categorised as Political, Economic, Social and Technological (PEST).

❑ Finally, we looked at how companies can organise their marketing activities – along functional, product or market lines.

The rest of this book looks in more depth at the marketing mix, and especially the inter-relationship between the elements of the mix. It also considers marketing research and marketing strategy.

## Further reading

CIM Study Text, Certificate, *Marketing Fundamentals* (BPP Publishing, London, 1994), Chapter 1.

G Lancaster & L Massingham, *Essentials of Marketing* (McGraw-Hill, London, 2nd edn, 1993), Chapters 1–3.
   This is probably the best general marketing text available, and students who wish to take their studies of marketing further are encouraged to read this book.

M J Baker (ed), *The Marketing Book* (Butterworth-Heinemann, Oxford, 2nd edn, 1991), Chapter 1 (M J Baker).

## Exercises

*Progress questions*

*These questions are designed to help you to remember the key points in this chapter. The answers are given on page 89. Complete the following sentences.*

1   Marketing is a ............................................................................ process.

2   The four elements of the marketing mix are ..................................................................

3   The macro environmental factors to be considered in marketing decisions are ........

...................................................................................................................................

4   The three ways in which a marketing department can be arranged are by ...............

...................................................................................................................................

Select the correct response to the following statements:

5   Marketing can be best summed up as advertising.

True ☐ False ☐

6   The four elements of the marketing mix have no effect on each other.

True ☐ False ☐

7   The macro environmental factors are only of interest to companies entering new markets.

True ☐ False ☐

8  A product manager may be marketing the same product in several different markets.

True ☐ False ☐

*Review questions*

*These questions will help you to check your understanding of the key concepts in this chapter. The appropriate section of this chapter is noted at the end of each question.*

9   Define 'marketing'. (Section 1.2)

10  What activities fall under the term 'promotion'? (Section 1.3.2)

11  What is meant by 'place'? (Section 1.3.4)

12  Draw an organisation chart for a company with a product-based marketing department. (Section 1.5.2)

*Multiple choice questions*

13  A marketing orientation means that

a)  a company looks to satisfy customer needs
b)  a company wants to be market leader
c)  a company has a good salesforce
d)  a company operates in many different markets.

14  Typical social factors to consider when looking at the macro environment include

a)  the average size of the family
b)  the type of government in power
c)  the proportion of wealthy people
d)  the automation of the industrial base.

15  The most common way of organising a marketing department is by product managers because

a)  it is the cheapest method
b)  it is the most effective method
c)  the product manager does not need to know about different markets
d)  advertising, marketing research, sales promotion and other activities are best done by outside agencies.

*Practice questions*

16  Explain how the elements of the marketing mix are inter-related.

17  Explain why it is important to consider the macro environmental factors when making marketing decisions.

18  Explain the shortcomings of a function-based marketing department.

*Questions for advanced students*

19  List the macro environmental factors that will need to be considered by a manufacturer of jams and a manufacturer of industrial pumps.

20  Using examples, show the inter-relationship of the elements of the marketing mix.

21  Taking your own company as an example, explain why you think the organisation of the marketing department is right or wrong.

## Assignment

It has been said that marketing is too important to be left to the marketing department.

What do you understand this statement to mean? Do you think it is true or false? Give reasons for your answer.

# 2 The product

## 2.1 Introduction

This chapter looks at the role of the product in marketing. Throughout this chapter (and indeed in this book) the term 'product' is used when talking about what is conventionally believed to be a product and also a service. A lot has been written about both the differences and the similarities between products and services, but for an introductory text it is easier to assume that they are one and the same.

The first area to be covered by this chapter is the product itself, from its physical reality to the benefits derived from its use. Next to be considered is new product development, an essential process by which companies renew and invigorate their offerings to the market place. The final subject is the product life cycle, a well used (but too often little understood) tool of the marketeer. By the end of this chapter, the student should

❏ know and understand different product types

❏ understand the difference between 'benefits' and features, and how the benefits are an intrinsic part of the product.

❏ know what constitutes a genuine 'new' product

❏ understand some of the basic strategies available to manage a company's product portfolio.

## 2.2 What is a product?

Products divide into two main types and three different categories. The types are 'consumer' and 'industrial'. Consumer goods are purchased by the end user, while industrial goods are used in the manufacture of a further product, which may then itself be sold to the end user or used in the manufacture of another product. The different categories are

❏ product class, such as washing powder or soft drinks or instant coffee

❏ product forms, such as biological or fizzy or granulated

❏ product brand or make, such as Persil or Coca-Cola or Nescafé.

### Activity 1

Divide the following into consumer goods and industrial goods:

a 100 gram jar of coffee

a dry cleaning service in a local high street

a lorry load of moulding sand for the foundry industry

a gallon of petrol

In most cases, the definition as either consumer or industrial is quite straightforward, but in some cases this is not the case. The following two sections should help to explain the difference between consumer and industrial goods.

### 2.2.1 Consumer goods

Consumer goods are purchased by the ultimate end user (or the person who does the shopping for the end user family). They can be sub-divided into three classes: convenience goods, shopping goods and specialty goods.

#### Convenience goods

These are items where very little thought is required before the purchase, and very little effort is required to make the purchase. They consist of the sort of goods purchased on a weekly basis at the local supermarket, petrol for running the family car, simple clothing items – in fact the everyday goods that most of us take for granted. Many products in this class are called FMCG (Fast Moving Consumer Goods), which covers such products as butter, breakfast cereal, washing powders, indeed the contents of a typical supermarket trolley.

Convenience goods can be further broken down into three sub-categories:

☐ staple goods, for example foodstuffs and items that are purchased regularly and repeatedly

☐ impulse goods, which are purchased without pre-planning such as a bar of chocolate when buying a regular (staple) newspaper

☐ emergency goods which are bought to satisfy an immediate need, such as a film for a camera at the entrance to the safari park.

#### Shopping goods

These can be defined as the sort of goods where, before buying, the prospective purchaser, will do some 'shopping around'. Comparisons will be made between product quality and price, post-purchase service levels, guarantees, and any special payment terms that may be available. Typical goods in this class include 'white goods' such as refrigerators and dishwashers, package holidays, non-basic clothing and cars.

#### Specialty goods

These goods could be characterised by the slogan 'don't accept imitations'. By their very nature they are special, and may require a lot of effort on behalf of the consumer to purchase them (if only because so few outlets stock them). They will inevitably command high prices. Examples of specialty goods include Rolex watches, *haute couture*, gold taps for the bathroom, and dinner at a top chef's restaurant.

## Activity 2

Classify the following as convenience, shopping or specialty goods:

a loaf of bread

a 60ft yacht

a pair of blue jeans

a family saloon car

a Rolls Royce

a packet of razor blades 2

### 2.2.2 Industrial goods

Almost by definition, industrial goods are involved in the production of other (ultimately consumer) goods. They can also be divided into three categories: capital goods, raw materials and components, and supplies.

#### Capital goods

These are the plant and equipment that a company needs to make its products or deliver its service. They are seldom bought without extensive deliberation, involving comparison of alternatives and investigation of after sales support and service. Goods that fall within this category include machine tools, heat treatment furnaces, process plant and earth moving equipment.

#### Raw materials and components

Raw materials, as the name implies, are products that are used in the production process. Examples include coffee beans to make instant coffee, sand for glass making, wool for making cloth for suits, and water for making beer.

Components may be taken as a step or two down the line from raw materials, in that they are 'things' rather than commodities, but they also go to make up the finished product. Thus components comprise such goods as automotive light fittings for assembly into cars, a pump assembly for incorporation into a central heating system, and a cathode ray tube for a television set.

#### Supplies and services

This category covers all those items that a company requires to keep it functioning, but are not directly used in the production process. For example, office stationery, light bulbs, floppy discs and catering services.

### 2.2.3 Benefits and features

The concept of the 'benefits' of one product over another is very important in marketing, and it is frequently used when promoting a product to its intended market.

A benefit is something about a product that makes it especially appealing to a potential purchaser. As an example, consider the choice of holiday destination. Principal benefits of choosing a particular location may include short flight time, guaranteed sunshine, good nightlife, good cultural activities, good food and so on. Thus different people will see different benefits in different holiday locations (and what will be benefits to some will be of no concern, or possibly even drawbacks, to others).

One way of distinguishing the benefits from the other attributes is to ask the question "...which means that...". For example, "My coat has a reflective strip on it ... which means that ... it stands out in car headlights at night ... which means that ... car drivers will see me ... which means that I won't get run over if I'm out at night wearing my coat." Thus a 'feature' of my coat is a reflective strip, but the benefit is increased safety. As another example "This drill bit has a tungsten carbide tip ... which means that ... it is harder than other drill bits ... which means that ... it will drill more holes before it goes blunt ... which means that ... it is cheaper per hole drilled." Thus the feature is a tungsten carbide tip, but the benefit to the consumer is cheaper holes.

## Activity 3

What do you believe are the benefits to the consumer/user of the following products:

a beer can containing a 'widget'

animal-shaped spaghetti

four hour video tapes

perfume

## 2.3 New product development

### 2.3.1 What is new?

Just as no one wants yesterday's newspapers, so very few people want yesterday's products. The pressure on companies supplying all market sectors, from industrial raw materials through to throw-away knick-knacks and confectionery bars, to produce new products is intense, if only because if Company A does, then Company B almost certainly has to in order to stay competitive.

How companies do this varies, but many larger organisations use both Research and Development (both internally and using outside agencies) and acquisition of other companies, patents or licenses.

A definition of what is truly new is probably very subjective, but the following definitions (produced by US Management Consultants Booz, Allen & Hamilton in 1982) are usually accepted in marketing:

a) 'New to the world', creating an entirely new market.

b) 'New product line', enabling a company to enter an existing market for the first time.

c) 'Additions to existing product lines' that complement established products.

d) 'Improvements/revisions to existing products' with new products that give improved performance and so replace existing products.

e) 'Reposition existing products' so that they appeal to new market segments.

f) 'Cost reduction' to provide similar performance at a lower price.

Most companies will use a mix of these strategies in order to try to minimise the risks involved.

### Activity 4

Into which definition of new would you put the following:

a) Ford Mondeo

b) paperback editions of books

c) Sony Walkman

d) special tariff mobile phones

e) biological washing powders

f) own brand cola drinks

### 2.3.2  The risks of new product development

As mentioned above, new product development is seen as high risk, and there have been some dramatic new product failures. These include the Sinclair C5 and the Persil Power detergent.

The causes of new product failure include:

a) overestimating the market size (i.e. not enough of the new product can be sold to cover costs)

b) the product doesn't do what the consumers expect it to do

c) competitive pressures are too strong creating excessively high barriers to entry

d) the advertising is wrong, the price is too high or the targeted market segment is wrong for the product

e) the product is not supported by distributors, stockists, dealers etc.

f) market research findings (pointing to lack of demand for the product) are ignored

g) competitors copy the product but also make improvements, thus making the initial product inferior and thus unattractive to the market.

In addition to these causes of new product failure, the risks involved in new product development are increasing. This is because consumers are becoming more demanding; competition is increasing (from all parts of the world); markets are more fragmented and each fragment requires its own marketing strategy; product life cycles are shortening and so payback times are decreasing; and the pace of technology is increasing, so what is 'state-of-the-art' at one moment can be quickly superseded by the next 'state-of-the-art' product.

### 2.3.3  The new product development process

Having considered the risks and the likely causes of new product failure, prudent management will put in place an approach that minimises risk and ensures that only the best ideas are launched into the market.

The Booz, Allen & Hamilton study referred to earlier identified eight stages of new product development.

i) Idea generation

The search for new ideas should not be casual, and must be guided by the company's overall objectives for new products. These could be related to cashflow, market share, risk reduction or technological advance. A system is needed to generate new ideas, which may come from customers, sales staff, research and development departments, distributors, service engineers etc. The important thing is that all the ideas thrown up by these different groups are considered by whoever has ultimate responsibility for new products.

ii) Screening

Of all the ideas generated and considered, many will be rejected at this screening stage. Reasons for rejection may be that the proposed project will not fulfil the company's stated objectives or it is too far from the organisation's core business. Often new product ideas are ranked for various criteria they would be expected to fulfil, for example complementary with existing products, anticipated return on investment, ease of manufacture, availability of raw materials, effect on competitors. Only those ideas that score sufficiently well are allowed to progress. Sometimes products pass this stage when they should not, and equally some worthwhile ideas are dropped (to be taken up by other companies).

iii) Concept development and testing

The idea has been generated and passed the initial screening process. It is then necessary to turn the idea into something more tangible that potential consumers can relate to. At this stage, the product concept should be tested on the potential consumers: would the product fulfil a need, are other similar products available, is the likely price realistic, and most importantly, would consumers in the target group actually buy the product.

iv) Marketing strategy

Once the proposed product and consumer reactions to it are fully understood, it is necessary to plan how to introduce the product to the market and how to sustain it at the required level of sales. The strategy document should cover all four elements of the marketing mix as well as sales and profit forecasts. It should also include an analysis of the market and the target consumer.

v) Business analysis

With the product concept fully developed and a marketing strategy in place, it is possible to consider the proposed new product from a business point of view. The two most important questions that need to be answered concern likely sales and likely costs and profits. It is not the intention of this introductory text to go into further detail on these questions, but suffice it to say that the importance of a full business analysis cannot be over-emphasised. Depending on what the numbers say, the proposed new product will either be dropped, or move on to the next stage.

vi) Product development

The money spent in the preceding stages will be small compared to what is now required. The product goes from being an idea to being a physical reality. The product must be as close as possible to the envisaged finished result, otherwise the results of the next stage (test marketing) will be meaningless. Depending on the type of product, extensive testing may be required for safety purposes (e.g. pharmaceuticals or cars) or for taste (e.g. new snack bars). In addition, production facilities will be required.

vii) Test marketing

Once the product exists and has satisfied any legal and safety criteria, it can be tested in the marketplace. This is usually done in a geographic area which is, as far as possible, representative of the population as a whole yet contains a sufficient number of the target market. The product may also be released to selected stores and other outlets, and the sales team will be briefed to record as much information as they can about customer reactions during this stage. Many lessons can be learned from test marketing, and they will be applied in the run up to the full launch.

viii) Commercialisation

If the product gets through its test marketing stage, there are four factors to consider before the full launch:

a) when – should the company be first into a new market or delay until a competitor has 'tested the water'?

b) where – regional, national or international, or a rolling programme from one region to the next?

c) target markets – who are the most likely consumers of the product (based in part on the test marketing results) and how can they best be persuaded to purchase it?

d) how – a launch action plan will be needed?

Thus the process of new product development can be long, and for every product that is successfully launched, many more will have failed and been withdrawn somewhere during the process. It also happens that products that pass all the tests and are launched into the market can fail.

So although new product development is essential if a company wishes to exercise any market leadership, the risks can be very great.

## Activity 5

a) How are new products developed in your company? Do you follow the eight stages outlined above?

b) Can you list some successful and some unsuccessful product launches from the last 10 years?

## 2.4 The product life cycle

The product life cycle is a fundamental part of marketing strategy. At the heart of the idea is the concept that all products have a definite lifetime, and that different strategies can be applied during different stages of the lifetime. The problem, of course, is that at the outset the lifetime of the product is unknown.

Figure 2.1 illustrates the product life cycle, and the four stages through which a product will pass.

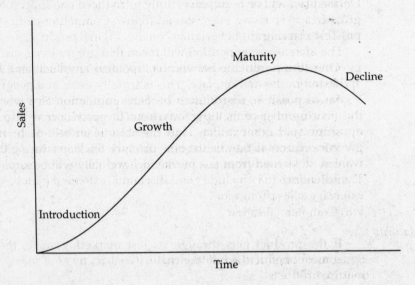

*Figure 2.1 Product life cycle*

The length of each stage is not fixed, and is dependent upon such factors as competitor activity, the market and macroenvironmental factors.

It must also be noted that the product life cycle applies to the product as a whole, and not to individual brands of that product. Thus if a supermarket chain decides to market its own brand of baked beans, it will not be introducing a product to the introduction phase, but to the maturity phase. Although own-brand baked beans are a new product for the supermarket chain, to the market they (the baked beans) are a mature product. In marketing terms, the baked beans are a product class.

The importance of the product life cycle to Marketing is the strategies that are adopted in each phase, and it is worth looking at these in more detail.

### 2.4.1 Introduction phase

The difficulties of launching a new product cannot be overemphasised – a new market has to be told about the product and educated about its use, the salesforce has to be trained to sell it, distributors have to be persuaded to handle it and retailers to stock it, and the product may need to be modified in the light of consumer response. On the plus side, there is likely to be very little competition.

In the introduction stage there is likely to be high expenditure on promotion in order to make the market aware of the product. This will involve advertising and sales promotion – advertising to create awareness and sales promotion to offer inducements to try the product (see Chapter 3).

There are classically two pricing policies for new products – penetration or skimming. A penetration policy means setting a low price in order to build market share. It is particularly appropriate when competitors are likely to enter the market with similar products.

A skimming policy means setting a higher price, allowing the development and launch costs to be recovered as quickly as possible. The high price can, of course, be reduced later in the product's cycle.

### 2.4.2 Growth stage

Once a product has been successfully introduced and is accepted by the market, rapid growth, and so rising sales, should follow. Competitors will start to enter the market, possibly offering slight variations on the original product.

The increased competition will mean that promotional spending will remain high, in order to differentiate between competitors' products and build brand awareness and loyalty.

As sales rise, so distribution becomes important. Any bottlenecks or hold ups in the process of getting the goods from the producer to the consumer presents an opportunity to competitors. Thus distributors and stockists/retailers will need to be given incentives to handle the new product. Shelf space is precious, and retailers only want to stock items that are, or they believe will be, successful and give good returns. The incentives may include good discounts, extended periods to pay, and evidence of extensive sales promotion.

### 2.4.3 Maturity stage

Since most products are in the maturity stage, most of marketing is concerned with mature products.

The size of the market is more or less static during the maturity phase, with growth or decline possibly reflecting the population demographics.

This stage is often marked by price reductions with the aim of holding existing market share or capturing share from competitors.

Another feature is continual refinements to the product and the introduction of similar products (i.e. broadening the product line) in an attempt to win new customers. For example, car manufacturers are continually refining the basic model and bringing out variations and special editions. Thus the Ford Escort exists in many different forms, all slightly different and appealing to a different market segment. Also computer software producers keep improving the basic programme and passing this onto existing users for a fraction of the price of a new package.

Promotional strategy will again emphasise the difference between the different brands available and try to build brand loyalty.

### 2.4.4 Decline stage

Eventually and for a number of reasons including consumer taste and technological advance, sales of all products will decline. They may not drop to zero, but any sales that are left are likely to be served by 'nichers'.

It should be noted that during the decline stage, the total market size (and thus level of sales of all supplying the market) is reduced. If the market size is staying the same but Company A is suffering a fall in sales, then there is some other cause, other than the product reaching the decline stage.

The major decision to be made during the decline stage is when to leave the market and drop the product. A fundamental concern will be the question of costs versus income, and when the cost of staying in a declining market exceeds the income from that market.

## Activity 6

Where would you place the following products in terms of the product life-cycle:

mobile phone

personal pension plans

Rubik cube

laser discs.

### 2.4.5 Special cases of the product life cycle

Not all products fit the classic product life cycle, which is one of the major criticisms of it (others being that it is never very clear where one phase ends and another begins, some 'products' will decline while the product class lives on, and the life cycle can be extended by finding new uses for a product).

Figure 2.2 illustrates the PLC for a 'fad' such as merchandising related to a popular film. The introduction period is very short but so is the maturity period of high sales. The decline is then steep and usually absolute.

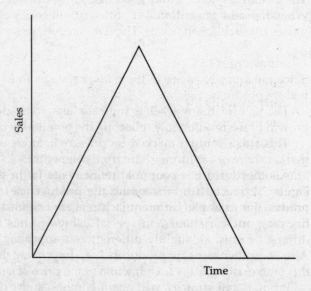

*Figure 2.2  Product life cycle for a fad*

Figure 2.3 illustrates the PLC for a product which is continually finding new uses or new markets. An example of a product following this pattern of behaviour is Coca-Cola. New market segments have been exploited for this drink, and those who drank it as children still drink it as adults and introduce their children to it. The Coca-Cola company also expands into overseas markets, with all the potential they offer for starting the whole process over again.

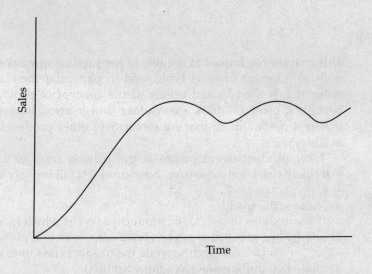

*Figure 2.3  Product life cycle for a product finding new uses or markets*

## 2.5  The product adoption process

When a product is introduced, different categories of consumers will purchase it as it passes through the life cycle. The five categories are:

innovators (2.5%)
early adapters (13.5%)
early majority (34%)
late majority (34%)
laggards (16%)

This is illustrated in Figure 2.4, which is similar in shape to the product life cycle in Figure 2.1. Just as different marketing strategies are required during the phases of the product life cycle, so different strategies are needed for consumers in each of these five categories.

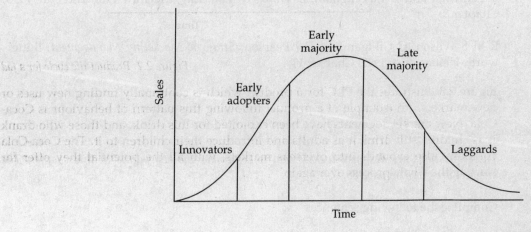

*Figure 2.4  The product adoption process*

## 2.6 Summary

This chapter has looked at the role of the product in marketing. It started with definitions of different product types, and in particular the classification as consumer or industrial. It then looked briefly at the concept of product benefits. The particular benefits a product offers a consumer (lower price, longer life, easier use) are what makes it preferable to that consumer over other products offering to fulfil the same needs.

New product development is the driving force of business survival, but also extremely risky and expensive. New products fall broadly into three categories:

a) new to the world

b) variations of existing products

c) new to the company making it.

New product development is a staged process, going through idea generation, initial screening, concept development, outline marketing strategy, business analysis, product development, test marketing and commercialisation. Inevitably, not all new product ideas will make it all the way from an idea to full commercialisation, as they fail at one of the testing points.

Finally this chapter considered the product life cycle, which is an attempt to track a product from its introduction to a market, through its growth in sales, its maturity and its eventual decline as demand for the product falls. As a product moves through the cycle, different strategies are needed for promotion, for pricing policy, for distribution, for management of the product and to attract consumers in the five categories of the product adoption process. The product life cycle has its critics, but so far no one has come up with anything better.

## Further reading

P Kotler, *Marketing Management*, Prentice-Hall, 7th edn, 1991, Chapters 12 and 13.

G Lancaster and L Massingham, *Essentials of Marketing*, McGraw-Hill, 2nd edn, 1993, Chapter 8.

R M S Wilson, C Gilligan and D J Pearson, *Strategic Marketing Management*, Butterworth-Heinemann, 1992, Chapter 11.

## Exercises

*Progress questions*

*These questions are designed to help you to remember the key points in this chapter. The answers are given on page 89.*

Complete the following sentences:

1   The two main types of product classification are ...........................................................

2   More thought is required when buying 'shopping' goods than 'convenience' goods because ...........................................................

3   The causes of new product failure include .................................................................

4   The eight stages of new product development are .......................................................

5   The four stages of the product life cycle are ............................................................

6   A penetration pricing policy when introducing a new product involves .................

   ..............................................................................................................................

Select the correct response to the following statements:

7   All consumer products can be bought in a typical shopping centre.

                                                        True ☐ False ☐

8   Raw materials are the only industrial goods.

                                                        True ☐ False ☐

9   The benefits offered by a red Ferrari include being red.

                                                        True ☐ False ☐

10  The only 'new' products are those that have never been seen before.

                                                        True ☐ False ☐

11  The first stage of the product development process is to establish a marketing
    strategy.

                                                        True ☐ False ☐

12  Most products are in the decline stage of the product life cycle.

                                                        True ☐ False ☐

*Review questions*

   *These questions will help you to check your understanding of the key concepts in this chapter.*
   *Other sources (e.g. from the Further Reading list) will help you to provide a fuller answer. The*
   *appropriate section of the chapter is noted at the end of each question.*

13  Describe the difference between convenience, shopping and specialty goods, as
    applied to consumer products. (section 2.2.1)

14  Explain using examples, how, as one of the 4 Ps, product is related to promotion,
    price and place.

15  For two competing products of your choice, outline the benefits each offers to the
    consumer. (section 2.2.3) (NB it is possible that the benefits will be, or appear to
    be, very similar.)

16  Explain what is meant by a 'new' product. (section 2.3.1)

17  Describe the eight stages of new product development. (section 2.3.3)

18  What is the product life cycle? (Section 2.4)

*Multiple choice questions*

19  The first stage of the new product development process is:

a)  research
b)  idea generation
c)  business analysis
d)  test marketing
e)  production

20  Most products are in which phase of the product life cycle:

a)  introduction
b)  growth
c)  maturity
d)  decline

21  One of the following is NOT a cause of new product failure:

a)  incorrect market size estimate
b)  the price is too high
c)  too many competitors
d)  no support from the retail trade
e)  the product is only available from very few retail outlets

*Practice questions*

22  Explain how consumer goods differ from industrial goods.

23  Describe the different categories of 'new' products, with at least one recent example in each.

24  Why do so many new products fail?

25  What factors does a company need to consider before launching a new product into the market?

*Questions for advanced students*

26  There are commonly held to be three types of consumer goods. Explain how they differ from each other.

27  How can a company generate ideas for new products?

28  Taking the mobile phone as an example, explain and describe the stages of the life cycle it has passed through.

## Assignment

You are the marketing manager of a medium-sized company making footwear (boots and shoes) for outdoor activities, in particular walking, hiking and climbing. Your newest product is over ten years old.

Although sales are still satisfactory, you are aware that your market share is slowly reducing.

### Required

Write a memorandum to your Managing Director explaining (a) why you believe that some new products are necessary and (b) what the process of new product development will involve for your company. You should consider:

i) new materials

ii) new uses for the footwear

iii) new market segments to look at

iv) idea generation

v) commercialisation

Any assumptions you make should be noted as such.

# 3 *Promotion*

## 3.1 *Introduction*

This chapter covers the subject of promotion of a product or service through the techniques of sales promotion, public relations (PR) and advertising. Sales promotion is often used as a short-term tactic to launch a product or shift surplus stock. Public relations is an ongoing dialogue between an organisation and its publics. Advertising, the most visible form of promotion, has a variety of purposes, the most common being to generate sales. In addition to examining these three activities in more detail, this chapter will also look at the process of communication and the relationship between the sender and receiver of messages, and the need for planning and control in the commissioning and execution of promotional plans. The term 'marketing communications' is used for these three activities in this chapter, as it is now well recognised that all these techniques are in fact communications between a company and its various audiences. Personal selling, an essential part of promotion, is considered in the next chapter.

By the end of this chapter the student should

❑ understand how communications work

❑ recognise the need for specific objectives for all marketing communications

❑ be aware of the different types of sales promotion

❑ understand the role of public relations

❑ know why companies advertise

❑ understand the factors to consider when advertising

## 3.2 *The process of communicating*

### 3.2.1 *The basics of communication*

Although marketing communications can take several forms, as mentioned in the introduction to this chapter, the basic process behind the communication is the same, and can be reduced to five variables:

a) the communicator, who sends the message

b) the content of the message

c) the audience for the message

d) the media via which the message is transmitted

e) the audience's response to the message.

The process of sending a message is illustrated in Figure 3.1. We see that, in simple terms, the sender (or communicator) encodes the message, sends it down a communication channel (the media), where it has to compete with noise, to the receiver (target audience), who has to decode the message using existing knowledge, cultural references and any other available information. There should then be feedback (audience response) back to the sender.

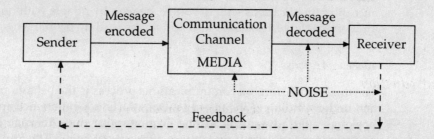

*Figure 3.1 A schematic diagram showing the process of sending a marketing communciations message*

### Communicator

The first variable is the communicator, which in this context is the company that wants to send a message. It is usually quite simple to find out who the communicator is, although some advertising works by not making clear the company behind it, the idea being to provoke interest by being mysterious. The communicator has control, to varying degrees, over variables (b), (c) and (d) but little over variable (e) other than by sending out effective communications.

### Content of message

The second variable is the content of the message (or communication) being sent. This message will have objectives which it wishes to achieve. The content will usually be either some sort of information (e.g. 0% finance and three years to pay; a new superstore has opened on the bypass) or an exhortation to do something (e.g. buy brand x; Keep Britain Tidy). The message should be as simple as it can be, while still giving enough information or being persuasive. As we shall see later, the communication is competing with a lot of extraneous noise.

### Target audience

The third variable is the audience at which the message is directed. The 'target audience' is one of the most important concepts in marketing communications. Most products and services are aimed at a specific target market and a lot of effort is expended in ensuring that the product will appeal to this market. Thus the 'target audience' for communications about international airlines will consist of (amongst others) business people who need to fly as part of their work, while the 'target audience' for particular package holidays may be families. For example, 18-30 holidays are aimed at fun-loving men and women in their twenties, and are advertised in magazines such people read. Golden Years holidays for the over sixties clearly have a different target audience and so a different type of advertising is used. Once the target audience is known, the fourth variable in the process can be tackled.

### The media

The fourth variable, referred to above, is the media used for transmitting the message. For example, advertisements for airlines appear in magazines such as The Economist, which is read by business people, and who are perceived as a group of people likely to need information about international airlines. Advertisements for package holiday companies, however, are more likely to appear in, for example, The Radio Times, which has a much more varied readership. However, 18-30 holidays may consider The Radio Times too staid, and use, e.g. Cosmopolitan to reach some of its target audience. Both publications will, of course, be read by people with no interest in the goods and services advertised, and also will not be read by people who do have an interest.

*Audience response*

The final variable in the communications process is the behaviour that follows receipt and understanding of the message. Does Airline X experience an increase in business bookings after advertising in The Economist, or does Package Holiday Company Y receive more enquiries from families after advertising in The Radio Times? The important point is that the communicator will have tried to obtain a specific response, and the success of the communication process is a function of the response of the audience.

We shall now look at two particular concerns of marketing communications: channel noise and the need for feedback.

### 3.2.2  Channel noise

The 'channel' is the method by which a message gets from the communicator (e.g. a company supplying goods or services) to the audience (e.g. actual or potential users of these goods or services). There are, however, many ways in which the message can be interfered with and which can hinder the receipt of the message by the audience.

These interferences may be as simple as poor printing of an advertisement in a magazine or poor positioning of it so that it is not easily seen amongst a lot of competing material. Channel noise is also caused when the audience is not concentrating on the message, for example making a cup of tea during the commercial breaks on television, or where the audience does not understand the message.

Methods of minimising the effect of channel noise include the following:

a)  getting the attention of the audience through effective creative ideas such as the use of colour, words or music

b)  the repetition of the most important part of the message, and

c)  research of the target audience to find out their tastes and attitudes so that the advertisement is relevant to the audience.

### 3.2.3  The need for feedback

As mentioned above, marketing communications should have defined objectives and it is therefore important to be able to judge if these objectives have been met. Feedback is the flow of information from the audience to the communicator.

Accurate feedback can be difficult to obtain, especially if the message was one such as "Keep Britain Tidy". However, it is essential if marketing management is to be able to answer the question "how successful was our last campaign".

Methods of obtaining feedback include monitoring sales of a product before and after a promotional campaign, questioning potential consumers or members of the target audience about their knowledge of the campaign, and attitude surveys of selected groups.

## Activity 1

Taking an advertisement of your choice, assess who or what you believe are the communicator, the message, the audience, the media and the desired feedback. Comment on possible channel noise surrounding the advertisement.

## 3.3  Planning and controlling communications

### 3.3.1  Integration with the marketing mix

As discussed in Chapter 1, the marketing mix consists of product, price, place and promotion. For marketing to be successful, the four Ps will support each other in such a way that one will seem perfectly logical and reasonable in relation to any or all of the others. Thus a high priced product will be sold in comfortable and exclusive surroundings (place), while a low priced product will be sold in a discount store, with little or no attempt at customer comfort.

The marketing communications must support the other three Ps. They must emphasise benefits of the product, they must support the price paid, and they must make the place where it is purchased seem right.

Thus expensive perfumes are advertised in glossy up-market magazines and sold in relatively exclusive stores. If advertisements for such perfumes started to appear in, for example, tabloid newspapers, the perfume manufacturers would not have such an exclusive product, and so would not be able to charge such a high price.

It is therefore most important when planning a communications strategy to consider the product that is to be promoted (and especially the benefits to the consumer of the product), the price that is to be charged, and the place and method of purchase.

### 3.3.2  Setting objectives

The need for specific, measurable, achievable, relevant and timed (SMART) objectives for all marketing communications campaigns cannot be stressed too highly.

Objectives must be specific – everyone involved with the marketing communications must understand them, e.g. increased sales.

Objectives must be measurable – the starting position or baseline must be known, and it must be possible, through sales records, enquiry records, or market research, to tell if the objective has been met, e.g. increased sales as measured by stock movement.

Objectives must be achievable – a 5% increase in sales is a target that can be achieved, e.g. increased sales as measured by stock movement by 5%.

Objectives must be relevant – what is relevant will vary with the product, but in many cases increased sales or greater awareness are relevant.

Objectives must be timed – a time limit must be applied, e.g. increased sales by 5% as measured by stock movement by 31 July.

Thus objectives are

Specific

Measurable

Achievable

Relevant

Timetabled.

If objectives are not set, then it is impossible to tell if the campaign has been a success or a failure. In addition, setting objectives at the start of the marketing communications process allows all those involved to focus their attention on how to meet them.

Thus the content of the message will be aimed at achieving a specific outcome, the best communication methods for achieving the objective will be chosen, and media planning can be highly targeted.

Marketing communications will be most effective when the goal is known and understood, and all involved are working towards the same goal.

The objectives for consumer oriented campaigns can be very varied, and the following list is by no means exclusive:

❐ to inform about a new product

❐ to increase use of a product

❐ to remind consumers of the existence of a product

❐ to inform consumers about special offers

❐ to show how a product should be used

❐ to build an image for the product

❐ to build brand loyalty.

The objectives for trade communications include the following:

❐ to inform the trade about the product

❐ to inform the trade about consumer communications

❐ to present special offers to the trade

❐ to explain to the trade how the product is used

❐ to build trade loyalty to the company.

Consumer and trade communications should work in concert, in a push/pull strategy. The producer of goods tries to push them down the distribution channel by offering incentives and information to wholesalers and retailers, for example by offering trade discounts or dealer competitions. The producer also encourages consumers to pull the goods down the channel by means of advertising and sales promotion. This is illustrated in Figure 3.2.

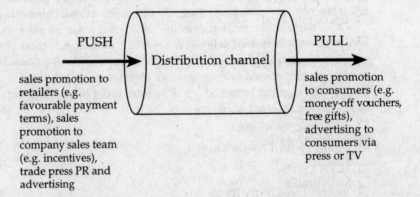

Figure 3.2 *Schematic representation of push/pull promotional strategies*

Needless to say, these objectives will require different promotional methods to meet them. The remainder of this chapter is devoted to three methods: sales promotion, public relations and advertising.

## Activity 2

You are the Marketing Manager of a medium sized engineering firm, providing specialist heating equipment to other engineering firms, who use it as a component in their products, to 'the trade', who sell it on to heating contractors and, to a lesser extent, the general public.

Your Managing Director has told you to "get a campaign together to sell some more".

Write a memo to the MD explaining, with reasons, the objectives you have set for future campaigns aimed at industrial customers, the trade and heating contractors.

## 3.4  Sales promotion

### 3.4.1  Advantages and objectives of sales promotion

Sales promotion is a short-term promotional tactic, providing an inducement to buy rather than trying to produce a long-term effect. Sales promotions can be very useful marketing tools because they are flexible, capable of specific action, not very expensive to implement, and fast acting.

Reasons for undertaking sales promotion include: the need to encourage retailers to stock the product, the need to move surplus stock, the need to motivate the sales force, and the need to back up advertising.

Before embarking on a sales promotion campaign, it is necessary to define the objectives and select the target audience as the first actions.

The target audiences for sales promotion activities and the objectives are closely linked, with there being three main audiences: consumers, retailers or trade, and the salesforce. The objectives for each of these audiences can include the following:

*Consumers*

- ❒ new product launch
- ❒ encourage trial
- ❒ encourage brand switching
- ❒ attract non-users

*Retailers/trade*

- ❒ encourage stocking
- ❒ guard against competitors
- ❒ build loyalty
- ❒ increase inventory levels

*Salesforce*

❏ increase order size and frequency

❏ encourage better display positions and better use of merchandising materials (in retailers)

To a large extent, these objectives are inter-related, from the salesforce to the retailer to the consumer, and a typical objective for a consumer goods based sales promotion may be:

To increase sales of product A by 10% in large retail stores and 15% in medium sized retail stores over the next two months by distributing sample products to selected households, offering discounts to retailers, and increasing in-store display of the product.

This objective has a time scale (two months), specific targets (10% and 15%) and methods aimed at consumers, retailers and the salesforce.

### 3.4.2 Methods of sales promotion

The methods of sales promotion obviously change depending on the target audience. The most common methods for the three audiences mentioned above are as follows:

*Consumers*

Price reduction (e.g. "5p off the recommended retail price")

The problem with this type of promotion is that firstly reverting to the old price at the end of the offer may be regarded as a price increase, and secondly regular users of the product may take the opportunity to stock up on the product at a reduced price, and so not need to buy the product for a while when it reverts to the 'real' price.

❏ *Gifts in/on packs*

This is often aimed at younger consumers, such as children influencing their parents to buy the breakfast cereal with the free gift in the pack or teenage magazines with free make-up gifts stuck to the front cover.

❏ *Coupons*

These are a form of money off, or price reduction, but the consumer must be in possession of the coupon, which may have been delivered to a residential address or cut from a magazine. Usually there will be a time limit and the coupon will be for a specific size of the product in question. This is likely to encourage purchase sooner than might otherwise have been the case, which helps (in the short term) with stock turnover. A problem with coupons is that many supermarkets (and other stores) will accept them for any products they stock irrespective of whether the consumer has purchased the product in question.

❏ *Free samples*

This is often used for new products and by new entrants into a market. The theory is that the consumer receives (often by door-to-door delivery) a small sample of a product, tries it, likes it and goes out to buy it.

❑ *Send aways*

This is the "collect five packet tops and then send away for your free gift of ..." method. This method obviously encourages re-buy, but many companies have been caught out when the demand has outstripped their supply of the gift. Sometimes re-buy can be further prolonged by having, say, five plates to collect, each requiring five packet tops.

*Trade promotions*

❑ *Discounts*

Quite simply, a percentage discount on the price for all cases (or similar) purchased. There may be a lower limit below which the discount does not apply. This encourages retailers to purchase more than they usually would. Also used in industrial situations (and by car dealers) with trade-in of old equipment for new.

❑ *Extended credit*

Giving retailers (say) 60 days to pay instead of 30 will be beneficial to them and is likely to induce them to look favourably on the company offering this.

❑ *Advertising allowance*

This is where a company will assist, say, its dealers with advertising in the local press. It is a method often used by car companies, who are well aware of the support they must give their dealer networks.

❑ *Exhibitions*

Exhibitions are an accepted part of business-to-business and industrial marketing, and in some industries to be absent from a trade exhibition is tantamount to admitting that the company is in serious trouble or is leaving that particular market. Exhibitions are a good opportunity to make new contacts and to reinforce the bond with old contacts.

❑ *Entertaining*

Used and abused in many areas of corporate life, this can include lunch with the 'rep' or an invitation to Wimbledon.

❑ *Free trial*

Again used in industrial situations, the prospective purchaser is allowed a free trial of the goods, in the expectation that they will then want to keep it.

*Salesforce promotions*

These are usually based on increased orders of the salesforce, and include prizes (e.g. weekend in Paris) for exceeding pre-set targets within the time limit. These salesforce contests will be over and above any commission paid for reaching the usual sales targets.

*Activity 3*

a) Still as the Marketing Manager of the medium-sized engineering company mentioned in Activity 2, outline sales promotion activities you could direct at your industrial and trade customers.

b) List some sales promotions that you believe are or have been successful and some that have not been, and give reasons for your verdict of successful or unsuccessful.

## 3.5 Public Relations (PR)

### 3.5.1 What is PR?

The Institute of Public Relations has described PR as "the deliberate, planned and sustained effort to establish and maintain mutual understanding between an organisation and its public".

The question of the different 'publics' a company confronts will be addressed later, but it must be realised that there is a difference between PUBLICITY and PUBLIC RELATIONS.

Publicity happens to a company and the company has no control over it. If a chemical company accidentally spills thousands of gallons of noxious chemical into a river, and it is the lead item on the local news, then that is publicity (and probably bad publicity). The company has no control over what is said and how it is presented. Public Relations may then be used to try to limit the damage.

Public Relations includes such activities as sponsorship of sporting events, Royalty opening a new factory, open days for customers, helping local good causes, in-house newsletters, and of course issuing press releases. Many of the activities that make up public relations will be aimed at more than one 'public', in so far as more than one public will be made aware of the company's activities.

Thus PR is deliberate, it is aimed at specific publics, and it has definite objectives.

### 3.5.2 The 'publics' a company must address

The publics include all those individuals, groups, and organisations with an interest or a stake in the company. They include the following:

The workforce – a well motivated and informed workforce that understands the company's mission is more likely to achieve its targets than one that is kept in the dark.

Shareholders – shareholders also need to be kept informed, and well informed shareholders who understand what the company is doing and where it is going are more likely to remain faithful if the going gets rough than shareholders whose only contact with a company is an annual dividend (with no explanation as to why it is less than last year's!)

Banks and other financial institutions – since a company may need money to finance capital expenditure plans, it is essential to be in regular contact with the likely source of the money.

Trade contacts (distributors and suppliers) – it is important to have good relationships with these two important groups. If the suppliers understand your company then they can adjust their service to suit your needs. The importance of giving both company and product information to all the members of the distribution chain cannot be overemphasised. This 'public' is buying and selling the company's products, and needs the knowledge to be able to do it well.

Consumers – for this particular public, PR is just one tool of the marketing communications mix, and must be co-ordinated with sales promotion, personal selling and advertising campaigns.

Media – often mistakenly thought of as the sole vehicle of PR, the media are used as one way of getting information to the other publics. It is thus important to have good relationships with the relevant trade press, and the business, local and national press, radio and TV (depending on the size of the company). Only authorised personnel should speak to the media.

### Activity 4

Outline the PR activities the company in Activities 2 and 3 could undertake, and the objectives of these activities.

## 3.6 Advertising

### 3.6.1 The reasons for advertising

Advertising is the visible part of marketing. All around us we see advertisements – on television, in magazines, on hoardings. In essence, advertising seeks to present the benefits of a product or service to the target audience in a way that is believable and appealing. The ultimate purpose of most advertising is to generate a sale, but it can have other purposes.

The typical reasons for advertising include:

❐ to generate sales

❐ to promote a brand

❐ to give an 'image' to a brand

❐ to improve the corporate image

❐ to create awareness of a (new) product

❐ to explain the benefits of a service

❐ to counter negative post-purchase feelings (i.e. to reassure consumers that they made the right purchase decision)

As with all promotional activities, it is important to set objectives, and it is when setting objectives that the various models of advertising/consumer behaviour can be useful.

### 3.6.2 The use of sequential models

So-called because the consumer is assumed to move through a sequence of stages on the way to a purchase, two sequential models will be considered here. It is worth noting that a lot of work has been done in this area, but the various models put forward all assume a hierarchy of effects (i.e. moving from one state or action to another).

The first model, put forward in the 1920s, is known as AIDA, and assumes a progression from Awareness to Interest to Desire to Action:

AWARENESS — INTEREST — DESIRE — ACTION

Thus an advertisement makes the audience aware of a product, it then excites their interest in the product or service, the audience next experiences a desire or want for the product, and finally the audience takes action by purchasing the product.

A second model was proposed in 1961 and is based on DAGMAR – Defining Advertising Goals for Measuring Advertising Results. Thus if specific goals (objectives) are set, it is possible to measure how effective advertising has been. This model assumes that the consumer moves through the stages of Unawareness to Awareness to Comprehension to Conviction to Action.

## UNAWARENESS–AWARENESS–COMPREHENSION–CONVICTION–ACTION

This model assumes that at first the consumer is unaware of a product, and so the first requirement of advertising is to create an awareness. Next the consumers must understand the product (comprehension) and then become convinced that it is the right product for them. Finally, the advertising must promote the required action, such as purchase of the product.

It thus seems logical that different advertising may be needed to move a consumer from one stage to another. First, informative advertising will be needed to tell the audience about a (new) product. The advertising will then need to become persuasive to achieve the desired action.

Although these models are useful as a guide to consumer behaviour and the effects of advertising, and so in helping to set objectives, it should be remembered that they are only models and consumers may not follow the prescribed sequences and may jump levels or even go backwards.

### 3.6.3  Advertising in action

As with the other elements of the promotional mix, there are a number of factors to be considered before embarking on an actual campaign:

a)  target audience

b)  objectives

c)  the message

d)  the media

e)  the budget

f)  measuring effectiveness

### Target audience

The first point to consider is at whom the advertising is aimed. This will partly be decided by the company's marketing strategy and market segmentation policy. The target audience must be tightly defined as many of the following decisions depend upon this. In addition, the audience must be understood, and their motives for purchasing a product should be known.

### Objectives

The second step is to set objectives. These should, of course, be quantifiable and have a time scale. The sequential models discussed above may prove useful here. Typical objectives may be to increase trial, to influence opinions, to generate direct leads for the sales team, and to affect behaviour.

*The message*

Once the target audience and the objectives have been selected and are thoroughly understood, the message that is to be conveyed to the audience can be considered. Obviously the message will be related to the objectives of the advertising, and it should be simple and believable. Advertising agencies can spend many hours and a lot of money deciding how the message can be best communicated, but if the message is put across in an inappropriate way for the product or in the wrong creative setting, then it will not do what it is intended to do.

*The media*

The next choice is the media to carry the message. This will be largely determined by the target audience (large or small, general or specialised, men or women, young or old), the content of the message, and the creative setting of the message. The choice of media breaks down into six areas: television, radio, cinema, newspapers (national and regional, plus supplements), magazines (consumer, trade and technical) and outside (i.e. billboards).

Thus certain messages which provide a lot of information (e.g. for pension plans) appear in newspapers, messages that need motion (e.g. for cars) appear on television, and messages that need colour (e.g. for foodstuffs) appear in consumer magazines. Above all, the media must reach sufficient of the target audience for it to be cost effective.

## Activity 5

Different media have advantages and disadvantages. What do you consider these to be for the six types of media for the following products:

- baked beans
- non-stick frying pans
- business class air travel
- a course on how to drive a steam train
- personal computers
- a shop selling wallpaper and curtain fabrics?

*The budgets*

Over and above all of these considerations is the budget. There are several common methods of setting an advertising budget: percentage of sales, competitor parity, and objective and task. The percentage of sales method has the disadvantage that brands or products that are selling well will receive a larger budget than products that are selling badly, which may be totally inappropriate. Competitor parity may be difficult to measure and may not be appropriate depending on relative market shares.

The objective and task method (i.e. set the objectives and then decide what must be done – the task – to meet them) is in theory the best way, but it does assume knowledge that certain actions (or tasks) will achieve certain results (or objectives). This may not always be the case as markets are dynamic with many variables (e.g. competitor's actions and general economic well being) to consider.

*Measuring effectiveness*

The final point to consider is how to measure the effectiveness of the advertising. For some types of advertising, e.g. ordering products directly by telephone or mail, or requesting a demonstration, this can be done relatively easily. For other types of advertising, and especially where the advertisements are seeking to change attitudes or opinions, measuring the response is more difficult.

There are, however, several ways of seeking to measure the effectiveness of advertising, including recall tests (in which respondents are asked if they remember advertisements that have recently appeared in the press or on television) and retail audits (which measure changes in sales during and after an advertising campaign).

---

### Activity 6

In the same role as in Activities 2, 3 and 4, outline who the target audiences are for your products, the message you would need to put across (bearing in mind your Managing Director's request to 'sell some more'), and the best media to use (in

---

## 3.7  Summary

This chapter has been concerned with the three main elements of Marketing Communications, i.e. Sales Promotion, Public Relations, and Advertising.

We have looked at the basics of communication and at the five variables to be considered (the communicator, the content of the message, the target audience, the media and the audience response).

The chapter next discussed the importance of objectives and how they must be clear, quantifiable, measurable and timetabled. A wide range of objectives is possible, with different objectives requiring different promotional methods to meet them.

Sales promotion is a short-term tactical method of inducing purchase rather than a long-term loyalty building strategy. Different sales promotion techniques can be used for consumers, retailers and the salesforce.

Public Relations is a deliberate and sustained effort by a company to communicate with, and make itself understood by, the 'publics' with which it comes into contact. The 'publics' include the workforce, shareholders and the media.

Advertising is the most visible part of marketing, and is used for a variety of purposes. One of the most important considerations before embarking on an advertising campaign is the target audience, and how best to reach them (i.e. what media to use). A message aimed at the wrong audience is simply a waste of money.

---

*Further reading*

CIM Study Text, Diploma: *Marketing Communications*, BPP Publishing Ltd, 1991.

M J Baker (Editor), *The Marketing Book*, Butterworth-Heinemann, 2nd edn, 1991, Chapter 19 (by K Crosier).

G Lancaster and L Massingham, *Essentials of Marketing*, McGraw-Hill, 1993, Chapter 11.

J Wilmhurst, *The Fundamentals and Practice of Marketing*, Butterworth-Heinemann, 1984, Chapters 8, 15, 16, 17.

## Exercises

*Progress questions*

*These questions are designed to help you to remember the key points in this Chapter. The answers are given on page 89.*

Complete the following sentences:

1   In marketing communications, the five variables of the communication process are .................................................................................................................................

2   Objectives should be ......................................................................................................

3   Sales promotion is a useful marketing tool because it is ..........................................

.................................................................................................................................................

4   A problem with 'coupons' as a method of consumer-based sales promotion is that

.................................................................................................................................................

5   The difference between publicity and PR is that ......................................................

.................................................................................................................................................

6   The media available to a company wishing to advertise are ...................................

.................................................................................................................................................

Select the correct response to the following statements:

7   The communicator has no control over who will receive the message.

True ☐ False ☐

8   If a marketing communications campaign does not have objectives, it can still be successful.

True ☐ False ☐

9   Sales promotions are only aimed at consumers.

True ☐ False ☐

10  The only 'public' of interest to a company is the people who buy its products.

True ☐ False ☐

11  The only reason for advertising is to increase sales.

True ☐ False ☐

12  Television is the best medium for all advertising.

True ☐ False ☐

*Review questions*

*These questions will help you to check your understanding of the key concepts in this chapter. Other sources (e.g. from the Further Reading list) will help you to give a fuller answer. The appropriate section of this Chapter is noted at the end of each question.*

13  Describe possible sources of channel noise in relation to advertising, and suggest how noise can be minimised. (Section 3.2.2)

14  Explain, using examples, how, as one of the 4Ps, promotion is related to product, price and place. (Section 3.3.1)

15  How does the setting of objectives (for any marketing communications campaign) assist those involved in the planning and execution of the campaign? (Section 3.3.2)

16  What problems may be encountered with a 'reduced price' sales promotion? (Section 3.4.2)

17  Explain why the media are only part of the 'public' that a company should communicate with through PR. (Section 3.5.2)

18  What is the purpose of the models of advertising/consumer behaviour? (Section 3.6.2)

19  Why is it necessary for an advertiser to understand the target audience at which the advertising is aimed? (Section 3.6.3)

20  What are the advantages and disadvantages of different methods of setting advertising budgets? (Section 3.6.3)

*Multiple choice questions*

21  The objectives of a promotional campaign must be:
    a)  quantifiable and verifiable
    b)  agreed by the Marketing Director
    c)  mentioned in advertising
    d)  easy to achieve

22  The reasons for undertaking a sales promotion exercise include:
    a)  building customer loyalty
    b)  rewarding the salesforce
    c)  encourage trial of a product
    d)  build up a large stock of a product

23  Public Relations can be defined as:
    a)  anything that appears about a company in the media
    b)  an effort to encourage mutual understanding between a company and its 'public'
    c)  holding an open day every now and then
    d)  counteracting bad publicity

24 The best place to advertise a product:
   a) is on television
   b) is in magazines
   c) depends on the target audience
   d) depends on the objectives

*Practice questions*

25 Explain the importance of the target audience when considering any form of promotional campaign.

26 Explain why all promotional campaigns should have objectives, and what criteria these objectives should fulfil.

27 Describe how sales promotion for one product can be aimed at consumers, retailers and the salesforce.

28 Explain the difference between public relations and publicity.

29 Describe the different methods of setting an advertising budget, and the advantages/disadvantages of each method.

*Questions for advanced students*

30 Explain how and why the sequential models of consumer action are used.

31 Compare the 'publics' a manufacturer of jams will have to consider with those that a manufacturer of industrial pumps will have to consider.

32 Explain how promotion integrates with the other elements of the marketing mix.

## Assignment

You are the Marketing Manager of a medium-sized company (employing 120 people) making a range of electric motors used in such applications as roller shutter doors, conveyor systems and small cranes. You advertise regularly in the trade press, exhibit at exhibitions, and entertain your best customers.

Your company has recently acquired a new Managing Director, who wants to know how you spend your time and the marketing budget. In particular, he wants to know if the desired results are being achieved or if the money could be better spent.

Required

Write a report to the new MD, explaining why you currently spend the promotions budget in the way you do. In particular you should consider:

i) objectives
ii) target audiences
iii) other marketing communication activities not already undertaken.

Any assumptions you make should be noted as such.

# 4 Selling as part of marketing

## 4.1 Introduction

It has long been debated whether selling is really part of marketing, or whether it is a completely separate activity. However, it is now generally accepted that selling is part of marketing, falling under the P for promotion. In many smaller companies, the sales and marketing functions are closely linked, usually coming under the overall control of one senior manager. In many larger companies, the two activities are distinct, often with a board level 'Marketing Director' and 'Sales Director'. This is not surprising given that the salesforce of a large company may be several hundred strong, and the marketing division may be concerned with new product development and putting together advertising plans.

It should be noted that in an industrial environment personal selling is of great importance. This is partly because advertising expenditure is likely to be relatively low, and partly because the technical nature of industrial products may mean that a lot of explanation is needed if the customer is to understand their merits and methods of use. In consumer markets, much of the selling is to the trade, with the final consumer being persuaded by means of advertising and sales promotion to try or continue to use a product.

So whatever the situation, selling, like the other aspects of marketing, is concerned with identifying customers' needs and wants, and then providing products or services to answer them.

By the end of this chapter you should:

❒ understand why personal selling is important within a company's marketing strategy

❒ understand the role of the salesforce

❒ be able to outline the selling process

❒ recognise the importance of the decision making unit in industrial situations

❒ know how the salesforce can be managed.

## 4.2 The importance of personal selling

There are three main reasons why personal selling is important:

a) Personal selling needs no other intermediaries from the introduction to the customer to accepting the customer's order (and possibly even taking the money).

b) Personal selling allows the customer's needs to be stressed, as a trained salesperson will be able to find out what is important to a particular customer and stress how the product he is selling can meet these needs.

c) Personal selling allows a two-way flow of information, with the company selling the goods able to gain valuable information about their customers' needs.

These reasons come strongly to the fore in industrial marketing, with the salesforce not only telling customers about their company's products, but tailoring their presentations to the customer's requirements. In such situations, the salesforce may also need to have sufficient technical knowledge to be able to answer detailed questions on the use or performance of the products being sold. Since every customer may ask different questions, it is obvious that in these cases personal selling is a far superior process to advertising.

## Activity 1

Why is personal selling important in industrial situations?

## 4.3 The selling process

Although no two sales interviews are likely to be exactly the same, most will be very similar and follow a familiar pattern:

a) planning

b) the initial approach

c) identification of the customer's needs

d) the presentation (and demonstration, if appropriate)

e) countering objections

f) negotiating

g) closing

h) after-sales service

In some instances, it may be possible to miss one or two of these components, or to pass over them very quickly because of the knowledge of the customer. They are, however, a useful checklist, and it is worth looking at them in a little more detail.

a) Planning

Although not strictly speaking part of the interview, adequate preparation is essential if the salesman is to have any chance of success. The importance of good record keeping will be discussed later in this chapter, but the salesman's records will often be the source of most information about a customer. The sort of information a salesman should have before calling on a customer includes:

> name and position of the person to be seen
>
> previous purchases from the salesman's company
>
> the customer's opinion of the salesman's company
>
> the buying company's business and real needs.

Good preparation also ensures that the salesman arrives at the stated time for the appointment with all the relevant brochures, leaflets, demonstration kit, and order forms.

b)  The initial approach

Appearances, whilst they can be deceptive, are extremely important at the start of a sales interview, especially if the buyer is not well known to the salesman. Thus tidy and clean hair, clean and well-pressed clothes, and clean shoes are essential.

The opening remarks made by the salesman to the buyer are also important, and may well set the tone for the rest of the interview. They would, of course, include the usual pleasantries and may also be related in some way to the reason for the meeting, or possibly something complimentary about the buyer's company.

c)  Identification of the customer's needs

Marketing is all about recognising needs and then fulfilling them. Once the salesman and the buyer have gone through the initial exchange of pleasantries and the conversation needed to create the right atmosphere, the salesman needs to find out more about the needs of the buyer and his company. More than one salesman has tried to sell product x to a customer, succeeded and then lost all subsequent business, because what the customer needed was product y.

It is therefore essential to establish the real needs (and not just the perceived wants) of the buyer and his company. This will, of course, mean asking questions, listening to and analysing the answers, before asking further questions to become certain of the real need.

The danger of seeking to ascertain the real needs is that the buyer will feel threatened, especially if the salesman concludes that what the buyer says he wants is not in fact the best product he could buy to do the job. A situation such as this obviously calls for tact and diplomacy.

d)  The presentation (and demonstration)

Having discovered the buyer's true needs, the salesman is able to ensure that his presentation addresses these needs. In particular, the salesman must emphasise the benefits of the product that meet the buyer's needs. In addition, the benefits that come from the salesman's product (as opposed to those from rival companies) should be stressed.

If appropriate, the product can be demonstrated. First, however, the salesman should explain how the product works, and how it should be operated. The demonstration should not take an undue length of time, and obviously the salesmen must be proficient at doing it.

All aspects of the presentation to the buyer must relate to how the benefits of the product will fulfil the buyer's needs.

e)  Countering objections

No matter how good the presentation, and how closely it dealt with the buyer's needs, objections may still be raised by the buyer. Often these will not be outright objections but rather requests for more information or requests for conclusive arguments in favour of the salesman's product.

Objections must be answered, and if the salesman is adequately prepared he is likely to be able to anticipate objections and provide a reasoned counter argument. Common objections can often be defused by the salesman referring to it in his presentation, and if possible turning what may be perceived as a weakness into a strength.

f) Negotiating

Many salesmen have the right to negotiate with the buyer on such issues as price, specification, delivery, trade-in, and credit terms. Careful preparation is essential before starting to negotiate on such matters as lowest selling price and what other options are open to the buyer. The two most important principles of negotiating are to start at a high but realistic level, and to give nothing away without receiving something in return (trading concessions).

g) Closing

Judging when to close a sale comes with experience, as does knowing the best technique to adopt. However, if the salesman does not close the sale, his rival may do so.

Sometimes the buyer will indicate that he is interested by asking about delivery times, colour schemes or credit terms. Other times the salesman may need to try a 'trial' close, such as asking the buyer what colour they would like, or when it would be convenient to make delivery.

Usually the salesman will wish to sum up the previous discussions, pointing out how the product meets the buyer's needs and the concessions that have been made, before asking for the order.

It may be necessary for the salesman to have a final concession to offer the buyer as a final inducement to placing an order, for example, extended credit or a small price reduction.

h) After-sales service

After-sales service may be as simple as a follow-up telephone call to confirm the delivery time, or to check that the product is working correctly. Or it may mean the actual servicing of a product (e.g. 6000 mile service for a new car). Whatever the case, good after-sales service is good PR, and companies ignore it at their peril.

## Activity 2

How can a salesman make sure he sells what the customer really needs?

## 4.4 The decision-making unit (DMU) in industrial selling

In industrial buying situations, there is rarely only one person who makes the decision of what to buy. A range of people will have an influence on the purchase decision, and the level of influence will vary depending on whether the purchase is:

a) a new buy, i.e. something that is totally new to the company

b) modified new buy, i.e. something that the company has bought before but has been changed in some way (possibly due to a switch to a new supplier)

c) habitual purchase, i.e. items the company buys on a regular basis.

Membership of the DMU will change as the items being bought change, but a salesman should try to identify the members of the DMU. Indeed, for large purchases it is vital that all the members of the DMU are identified and that the appropriate message is delivered to them.

Most DMUs will contain at least some of the following types of people:

a) The buyer: This is the person who writes out the order, and in large organisations may be dealing with dozens of purchases each month. With habitual purchases their influence is very strong (and indeed they may not need to refer to anyone else), but in new buy situations their influence will be very small.

b) The user: Most companies will at least consult the person who uses or will use the product. Depending on their status and the product or equipment to be purchased, users can have a lot of influence.

c) Influencers: These are people who although not actively involved in the buying process, and not actually going to use the product, can still influence the decision. They may be technical people or have some relevant specialist knowledge or experience.

d) The decider: The size of the purchase (in value terms) is likely to influence how far up in a company the purchase decision is made. It is thus not always possible for a salesman to meet or influence the decider, but he should try to find out who will make the recommendation to the decider.

e) The initiator: This is the person who first suggests getting some new equipment or materials. This person may then take ownership of the project and be the one who makes the recommendation to the decider from which company to buy.

f) The specifier: Many large companies, and particularly those involved in engineering and safety-critical activities, have written specifications for everything they purchase. If your product does not conform to the specifications, then you are extremely unlikely to be able to sell it to such a company.

Although the above refers mainly to industrial situations, the decision-making unit also functions within consumer buying and family groups.

---

*Activity 3*

What role, as part of a decision making unit, would members of a family (e.g. mother, father, teenage daughter, teenage son, younger daughter, younger son) play in the following decisions:

a) choosing a holiday destination

b) buying a new car

c) choosing a new carpet for

    i)   the living room

    ii)  the teenage daughter's room.

---

## 4.5 Sales management

Sales management can be divided into two areas: managing the salesforce and the organisation of sales.

### 4.5.1 Managing the salesforce

It is outside the scope of this book to look in any detail at how a salesforce can be managed, but is worth looking at the three most common methods of paying them. These are: fixed salary, commission only, and salary plus commission.

#### Fixed salary

This method of remuneration is particularly relevant to industrial selling, where it can take several months to secure an order. It is also useful when the salesman's job is not solely involved with selling but he is required to give technical service. Finally, the salesman will not be tempted to sell only those products that give a quick return, but can sell all the company's products secure in the knowledge that his income is guaranteed.

The disadvantages of fixed salary are that there is no direct financial incentive for the salesman to increase sales, and selling costs remain the same whatever the level of sales.

#### Commission only

The biggest advantage of commission-only remuneration is that the salesman's salary is dependent on his abilities to sell. However, in such cases the salesforce will be most reluctant to do anything that is not directly related to getting more sales, and the company has less control over the salesforce. For the company employing the salesforce, the cost of sales is linked directly to the volume of sales, and the level of commission on different products can be varied.

#### Commission plus salary

This attempts to amalgamate the best points of the other two methods, and thus provide an incentive to sell more with a level of security. The management can insist on some degree of non-sales related activities being undertaken, and yet the salesman can earn more money through his own efforts.

### 4.5.2 Organisation of sales

All companies with a salesforce need to consider how it will be organised, and will usually adopt one of three strategies: territorial, product or customer.

#### Territorial

In this method, a salesman will sell the full range of a company's products within a certain geographic area. If the product range is large, it may be impossible for the salesman to possess the necessary knowledge about all the products. On the plus side, the salesman is likely to be able to develop good relationships with his customers.

#### Product

With this method, each salesman is responsible for a specific product, or group of products. This has obvious strengths when dealing with technical products, but has the drawbacks that a lot of travel costs may be incurred, and may mean two or more salesmen visiting the same customer to sell different products from the range.

*Customer*

Customers can be differentiated in two ways: the industry they are in and the size of the account (i.e. large or small sales to that customer).

An advantage of differentiating by industry is that it allows the salesman to build up a detailed knowledge of the particular industry he serves.

The major advantage of differentiating customers by account size is that senior salesmen can deal with the largest and most important accounts, while more junior members of the salesforce can look after smaller accounts.

## Activity 4

**What are the advantages of the three different ways of organising a sales force?**

## 4.6 Summary

This chapter has looked at the basic aspects of personal selling. We have seen how important it can be within an industrial setting and we have gone through the various stages of the selling process. The importance of identifying the decision-making unit has been addressed. Finally this chapter has looked at different ways of managing the salesforce.

## Further reading

Alan Gillam, *The Principles and Practice of Selling*, Butterworth-Heinemann, Oxford, 1982.

G Lancaster & L Massingham, *Essentials of Marketing*, McGraw Hill, Maidenhead, 2nd edn, 1993, Chapter 12.

P Kotler, *Marketing Management*, Prentice-Hall, Englewood Cliffs, 7th edn, 1991, Chapter 24.

M J Baker (ed), *The Marketing Book*, Butterworth Heinemann, Oxford, 2nd edn, 1991, Chapter 1 (J Lidstone).

## Exercises

*Progress questions*

*These questions are designed to help you to remember the key points in this chapter. The answers are given on page 90.*

Complete the following sentences:

1   Personal selling is important because ...............................................................................

2   Typical information required by a salesman before a sales interview includes .........

....................................................................................................................................................

3   A 'trial' close of a sale can include ....................................................................................

4   The role of the 'influencer' in a decision-making unit is .............................................

5   The three ways of organising a salesforce are ..............................................................

Select the correct response to the following statements:

6   On meeting a potential customer, the salesman should immediately present his best product.

True ☐ False ☐

7   If a customer wants to buy a product, he/she will always say so.

True ☐ False ☐

8   The most important person in the decision-making unit is the decider.

True ☐ False ☐

9   The best way to reward the sales team is with a fixed salary.

True ☐ False ☐

*Review questions*

*These questions will help you to check your understanding of key concepts in this chapter. Other sources (e.g. from the Further Reading list) will help you to give a fuller answer. The appropriate section of this chapter is noted at the end of each question.*

10  Explain why personal selling is especially important in industrial situations. (Section 4.2)

11  Why is it necessary to identify the customer's real needs? (Section 4.3)

12  How can a salesman 'close' a sale? (Section 4.3)

13  How does the role of the DMU change in different industrial buying situations? (Section 4.4)

14  What are the advantages and disadvantages of fixed salary and commission only as ways of paying the sales team?

*Multiple choice questions*

15  The first step in a sales interview is
    a)  planning
    b)  the presentation
    c)  the initial approach
    d)  arriving on time
    e)  identifying the customer's needs

16 Which of these is not part of a DMU
   a) decider
   b) specifier
   c) operator
   d) initiator
   e) user

*Practice questions*

17 Explain why planning is important in the selling process.

18 Explain how the decision-making unit works.

*Questions for advanced students*

19 Explain the different steps a sales interview goes through.

20 Discuss the concept of the decision-making unit in consumer goods.

## Assignment

You are the Marketing Manager of a company supplying kitchen utensils direct to major stores. Your salesforce is currently organised on a regional basis and paid by salary only.

Your Managing Director wants the sales team to be paid on a commission-only basis.

Required

Write a memorandum to your MD defending the current method of payment. Your memo should cover the regional aspects of the organisation of the sales team, seasonality of demand, methods of controlling the workforce, and any other aspects you think important.

(If you agree with your MD, write a memorandum to the Regional Sales Managers explaining why the change would be a good thing.)

Any assumptions you make should be stated as such.

# 5 Pricing policy

## 5.1 Introduction

The importance of the price of a product or service changes in relation to the other elements of the marketing mix and also the general economic situation. Thus in times of low economic activity (e.g. during a recession) price becomes an important factor and may be the most important one when consumers choose between one brand and another. In boom times, price is less of a controlling factor, and consumers will consider other attributes of the product, for example, its social cachet or how it is advertised, rather than go for the lowest price. Thus price should always be considered alongside the other elements of the marketing mix, within the context of the company's overall strategy, and most certainly taking full cognisance of the market where the product will be offered.

By the end of this chapter you should

❏ understand the different objectives of pricing policy
❏ understand the relationship between 'costs' and price
❏ understand the factors to consider when setting a price
❏ know how pricing relates to the other elements of the marketing mix.

## 5.2 The objectives of a pricing policy

If the product on offer has been properly thought through, then the company will have identified the target market, have designed a product that will appeal to that market, have a promotional plan that will reach that market, and have the distribution channels in place ready to deliver it to that market. If this is the case, then setting a price ought to be relatively straight forward.

However, when setting the price, the company may be pursuing other, corporate objectives as follows:

### Survival

If a company is facing extinction, the most important objective is to keep cash flowing into it. Thus prices will be slashed (usually to below the full costs) simply to allow the company to continue to trade. Survival, needless to say, is a short-term objective, and if it continued for too long, the company will still go under. It should, however, produce sufficient breathing space for new products to be developed or new markets to be entered.

### Improve market share

Higher sales almost invariably mean lower unit costs (of production and distribution). To increase market share usually requires a price lower than that of the nearest competitors. This, of course, assumes that the market is price sensitive, and that a price cutting war does not break out, leading all the competitors to cut prices.

51

*Return on investment*

Many companies have a policy that all products are required to show a pre-determined rate of return on the investment involved in them. This requires the level of demand to be estimated and also the costs of meeting that demand. The price is then set to produce the desired profit (or return on investment). This method of pricing ignores the other elements of the marketing mix and the actions of competitors, and assumes that demand can be estimated accurately and that costs will remain constant.

## 5.3  Specific pricing policies

### 5.3.1  Market skimming

Market skimming is the name given to the tactic of setting a high price for new products. The advantage is that a company can quickly recover its development and start-up costs. The price is then gradually lowered as the market expands or new segments are entered. To be effective, the barriers to market entry need to be high (in terms of research and development) and there will need to be sufficient consumers prepared to pay the high initial price. Skimming cannot be tried in markets that are easy to enter, as competitors will simply undercut the price and still make a healthy profit.

### 5.3.2  Market penetration

The objective of market penetration is to ensure a high level of sales, as quickly as possible, by setting a low price. This is also used when launching new products, when the low price may deter competitors, or when entering new markets, when a low price is the only way to win market share from the established competition.

### 5.3.3  Product differentiation

A higher price than competitors can be set to emphasise the higher quality of a product. Also different products from a broad range are priced differently to appeal to different market segments.

### 5.3.4  Promotional pricing

Sometimes a company will price its products below the level the market expects, or competitors charge. There can be several reasons for this.

First, many supermarkets have 'loss leaders', products that are priced well below the market norm in an effort to attract customers into the store and so increase sales on other items.

Secondly, with expensive household goods companies may offer very low rates of interest or finance deals. This method of promotional pricing is very common with products such as cookers, three-piece suites and cars.

### 5.3.5  Psychological pricing

This pricing method takes two forms. The first involves setting prices below an artificial barrier, for example £1.99 or £99.99, rather than £2.00 or £100. The reasons for this are obvious, insofar as 'under £2' and 'under £100' are more appealing to consumers than 'exactly £2' or 'exactly £100'. If the price has to be increased through the barrier, then it should be by a reasonable margin, say to £2.20 or £108.00.

The second method of psychological pricing is to set a price that is much higher than the market is likely to stand and then offering a discount, e.g. "was £49.99, now only £34.99". Consumers are then expected to believe that they are getting a substantial reduction as well as obtaining a high-quality (because of its originally high price) product cheaply. There are, however, laws covering for how long and in how many outlets the product must be offered at the original price.

### 5.3.6 Discriminatory pricing

This is the method whereby products are sold at different prices depending on the customer group, location, or time of day.

For example, sports facilities may have different charges for families, students or children. Petrol is more expensive at a motorway service station than from a garage in town facing competition from supermarket petrol stations. And electricity companies change the price of electricity to large users during the day (reflecting the level of demand).

For discriminatory pricing to work, it must be possible to segment the market into the different groups to which the different prices will apply. Segmentation is discussed in Chapter 8.

### 5.3.7 Product range pricing

Again there are several elements to this particular pricing tactic. The first is concerned with product line pricing. This is seen most clearly in markets where a single product comes in several different versions, each more sophisticated (and 'better') than the one below. An example would be electrical goods such as televisions or HiFi's. A simple television may sell for £149, but as features such as Teletext are added, and the remote control becomes capable of doing more, so the price increases. To be successful, the price difference must be small enough to attract the consumer to the higher priced goods, but large enough to cover the extra cost to the company of making it.

The second important use of product range pricing is when the consumer needs to buy frequently used spares. For example, a decent ball-point pen is not too expensive, because the manufacturers know that the owners will have to buy refills that are specific to that brand of pen. The refills will have a high mark-up on them as the company seeks to make its profit from this area of its product sales.

## Activity 1

List some examples of discriminatory pricing and product range pricing.

## 5.4 The cost approach to pricing

The cost of producing any product can be split into fixed costs and variable costs. Fixed costs are those that remain constant irrespective of the sales volume. Variable costs increase as the sales volume increases.

## Activity 2

List some variable costs and some fixed costs in a typical manufacturing company.

Your list for variable costs should include raw materials, distribution, packaging, selling costs (which may show a decrease per unit but are likely to increase overall as sales rise, especially if the sales team are paid on a commission basis).

Fixed costs include rates, central overheads, promotional spending, labour costs, energy (lighting, heating etc.).

From this information it is possible to plot a break-even chart, as shown in Figure 5.1.

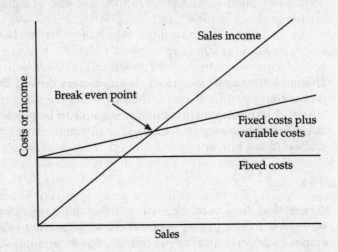

*Figure 5.1  Break even chart*

As we see from Figure 5.1, the fixed costs remain constant while the total costs (fixed and variable) rise as output rises. The usefulness of the break-even chart is that it allows the effect of different prices to be plotted to show at what level of sales they start to produce a profit. Equally the effect of altering the costs can be judged in terms of required sales to break even.

Knowledge of costs is important for two pricing methods – mark-up (or cost plus) and return on investment.

Mark-up pricing involves adding a fixed sum (or percentage) to the total fixed and variable costs to give the price charged to customers. The drawbacks of this method include ignoring competitive pressures and possible fluctuations in price owing to changes in raw material costs. This is, however, a common method of arriving at the price of both goods and services.

Return on investment pricing, as mentioned earlier, requires an estimate of the demand for the product as well as knowledge of the costs. The price to be charged can be worked out from the formula:

$$Price = Unit \ Cost + \frac{Percentage \ Return \times Capital \ Invested}{Sales}$$

This pricing method totally ignores market conditions, and may indeed come up with a price that is higher or lower than consumers are prepared to pay.

## 5.5 The marketing approach to pricing

The marketing approach to pricing considers more than just the cost of producing a product and getting it into the shops. Thus the company's overall marketing objectives will be taken into account (for example, is the company aiming for a high market share, which presupposes a low price in comparison to competitors or for a position of quality leadership which suggests a higher price than competitors). The other elements of the marketing mix will play a role (for example, the level of advertising support, the exclusivity or otherwise of the retail outlets at which the product appears, and the benefits that the product offers). The prices set by competitors will be analysed, and in many instances this will mean that similar products appear at very similar prices. Finally the nature of the market will be important, including the number of competitors supplying the same or similar products. If there are many, then price competition will be severe. In this case, companies will also attempt to differentiate their products by using other elements of the marketing mix.

## 5.6 Pricing during the product life cycle

The product life cycle was discussed in Chapter 2 and is illustrated on page 18. As a product passes through its life cycle, the pricing of a product has different objectives.

During the introduction phase, it is usual to set either a penetration price, to gain market share, or a skimming price, to recover development costs as quickly as possible.

In the growth stage more competitors will enter the market and it is likely that a 'going-rate' price will appear. This is due to competitors fixing their prices close to each other, with the result that consumers then accept this as the going rate. Any deviation from the going rate will be viewed with suspicion by consumers.

If the company entered the market with a skimming policy, it is likely during the growth stage to gradually lower the price as original costs are recovered and as new market segments adopt the product.

The maturity stage is usually marked by fierce price competition. The market is about as big as it is going to get (apart from growth caused by population growth) and extra sales can only be gained from competitors. Thus market share becomes all important, with price being one weapon in the bid to capture customers from competitors.

During the decline stage of a product's life cycle, prices may be cut further as companies attempt to retain their market share. When all but a very few companies have dropped out, prices may rise again as the product, which is still sought by some, becomes scarce.

> *Activity*
>
> List some products in the maturity stage of the life cycle that are the subject of price competition.

## 5.7 Summary

This chapter has considered pricing as a function of marketing. It has looked at different methods of pricing and at the cost elements to be considered when setting a price.

It then looked at pricing as part of marketing strategy, throughout the product life cycle and in relation to other elements of the marketing mix.

### Further reading

P Kotler, *Marketing Management*, Prentice Hall, Englewood Cliffs, 7th edn, 1991, Chapter 18.

CIM Study Text, *Certificate, Marketing Fundamentals*, BPP Publishing Ltd, London, 1994), Chapter 6.

M J Baker (Ed), *The Marketing Book*, Butterworth-Heinemann, Oxford, 2nd edn, 1991, Chapter 16. (J Winkler)

G Lancaster and L Massingham, *Essentials of Marketing*, McGraw-Hill, London, 2nd edn, 1993, Chapter 9.

### Exercises

#### Progress questions

*These questions are designed to help you to remember key points in this chapter. The answers are given on page 90.*

Complete the following sentences:

1   Market skimming pricing policy is the name given to the tactic of ..............................
................................................................................................................................................

2   Market penetration pricing policy is the name given to the tactic of ..........................
................................................................................................................................................

3   Some typical fixed costs are ........................................................................................

4   Some typical variable costs are ..................................................................................

5   In pricing terms, the maturity phase of the product life cycle is characterised by ....

.......................................................................................................................................................

Select the correct response to the following statements:

6   The objective of price is always to maximise profit.

True ☐ False ☐

7   Cost is the only thing to consider when setting prices.

True ☐ False ☐

8   It is necessary to be able to forecast sales accurately to set a price based on a fixed return on investment.

True ☐ False ☐

9   The growth stage of the product life cycle is characterised by large price differences.

True ☐ False ☐

*Review questions*

*These questions are designed to check your understanding of the key concepts in this chapter. Other sources (e.g. from the Further Reading list) will help you to give a fuller answer. The appropriate section of the chapter is noted at the end of each question.*

10  When might a company adopt a market skimming pricing policy? (Section 5.3)

11  When might a company adopt a market penetration pricing strategy? (Section 5.3)

12  Why is a break-even chart useful when considering price? (Section 5.4)

13  Explain how and why the approach to pricing changes during the product life cycle. (Section 5.6)

*Multiple choice questions*

14  Which of the following is *not* generally regarded as a fixed cost:
    a)  rates
    b)  heating
    c)  raw materials
    d)  director's remuneration

15  Which of the following is *not* generally regarded as a variable cost:
    a)  packaging
    b)  salesforce commissions
    c)  advertising spending
    d)  packaging costs

16  Which of the following is an example of discriminatory pricing:

    a)  theatres offering students reduced rates for Monday nights

    b)  was £9.99, now only £7.99

    c)  a litre of milk for 20p

    d)  set A, £250; set B, £320; set C, £430

*Practice questions*

17  If similar products are offered at similar prices, how can the consumer choose one from another?

18  Why might a company reduce the price of a product once it has been successfully introduced into the market?

*Questions for advanced students*

19  Explain how price integrates with the other elements of the marketing mix.

20  Using examples, explain how price can be used to differentiate products.

---

## Assignment

You are the Marketing Manager of a company supplying specialised chemicals to manufacturing industries. You have a reputation for quality, a loyal customer base, and only minor competition in your home market (a few companies offer some competing products).

However, an overseas supplier has entered your market and is pricing its products approximately 10% below yours.

Required

Write a memorandum to your Managing Director outlining what actions you should take. Your answer should consider ALL elements of the marketing mix and not just price.

Any assumptions you make should be stated as such.

# 6 *Place and distribution*

## 6.1 *Introduction*

The fourth 'P' of marketing is 'place'. This is usually taken to have a larger connotation than simply the physical place where products or services are sold, and also includes the methods of getting the product to the point of sale. These are known as 'Channels of Distribution', and are an important aspect of any company's marketing strategy.

It may be tempting to think of distribution as merely a logistical problem, simply a matter of getting the goods from the factory to the retailer (or possibly direct to the customer in an industrial situation). Equally it may be considered to be of no concern to the manufacturing company the environment in which the goods are sold. This chapter will show that both the channel of distribution and the place of purchase are important in marketing terms as the choice of these two factors will affect all other marketing decisions.

By the end of this chapter you should

❑ understand the different channels of distribution

❑ recognise the changes that have been taking place in channels of distribution and retailing

❑ understand the importance of channel intermediaries

❑ understand how different types of channels of distribution function

❑ know the criteria that need to be considered when considering different channels.

## 6.2 *Channels of distribution*

The purpose of a channel of distribution is to get products from the manufacturer to the consumer. This must be done as efficiently and as effectively as possible – no money should be wasted but the channel must be 'right' for the company's overall marketing objectives and strategy.

### 6.2.1 *The advantages of channel intermediaries*

In a simple world, a company makes a product and the consumer buys it direct from the manufacturer. That, however, is rarely the case. The manufacturer or producer and the consumer may be geographically separated. The consumer does not want to visit 50 different manufacturers in order to buy a week's groceries, and the producer does not want to deliver to all the outlets stocking the goods. The use of a middleman, or channel intermediary, contributes to efficiency, as the example in Figure 6.1 shows.

Thus without a middleman, a total of 12 contacts are required for each producer to service each customer. But with a middleman only 7 contacts are needed, which is more efficient for both producers and consumers.

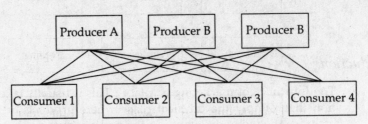

No channel intermediary – a total of 12 contacts

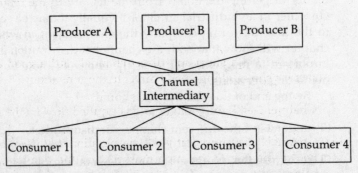

With channel intermediary – a total of 7 contacts

*Figure 6.1  The advantages of a channel intermediary*
*in reducing the number of contacts*

Channel intermediaries perform a variety of tasks, for example, providing variety for the consumer, breaking down bulk purchases into easily manageable quantities, assisting with promotional activities, and geographic dispersion.

In addition, retailers perform specific functions. For example, they hold a range of related products (cassette players and the batteries to power them, from a different manufacturer), they are able to display products in a way that makes them appealing to consumers, and they are in some cases able to offer advantageous financial terms to their customers ("0% finance and 12 months to pay").

### 6.2.2  *Types of channel intermediaries*

There are three types of channel intermediaries: agents, wholesalers and retailers. Some typical channels are illustrated in Figure 6.2.

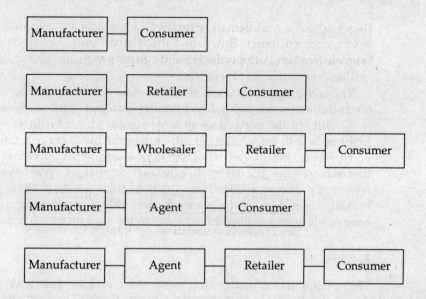

*Figure 6.2 Some typical distribution channels*

Channel 1 is a short and direct channel, and a good example of this would be a factory shop, selling goods direct to the consumer.

Channel 2 is slightly longer and is typified now by the supermarket grocery trade.

Channel 3 is representative of the situation that used to exist in retailing in the UK, before the rise of the supermarkets and the demise of the large regional wholesalers.

Channel 4 is typical of some direct sales operations. For example, Tupperware products are sold by agents to the consumer, although in this case the agent is never the actual owner of the goods.

Channel 5 is a typical export channel for a company that is only going into exporting in a small way, or which has a very specialised product that does not warrant an overseas sales team.

## Agents

Agents are used extensively in export markets, especially when the producing company does not have a detailed knowledge of the export market, when the producer's ambitions are limited, or when the level of sales does not make the cost of a full-time sales team worthwhile.

Agents usually work in one of two ways. First, they obtain orders from customers, pass these to the producer and then take a commission on the agreed price. The contract is between the producer and the customer although very often (and especially for industrial goods) the agent will build up a good relationship with the customer, to the mutual benefit of producer, customer and agent.

The second way for agents to operate is for them actually to purchase the goods from the producer and then sell the goods directly to consumers or to other channel intermediaries such as retailers. In such situations the agent will often be required by the manufacturer to hold a minimum stock level.

## Wholesalers

Wholesalers buy large consignments from producers and then sell the products in smaller consignments to retailers.

The advantages of the wholesaler system are that producers have reduced costs as fewer deliveries are needed and retailers can purchase products in the numbers they need, without the need to carry large stocks. This, of course, means that the storage problem is with the wholesaler rather than the producer or retailer.

However, the role of wholesalers is changing as supermarkets take on this role themselves. Thus the large supermarket companies now have regional distribution centres. Producers deliver lorry loads of their goods to these centres, the loads are broken down into consignments for individual supermarkets, and the supermarket company's lorries deliver mixed loads to the supermarkets in the locality.

## Retailers

The retailer has direct contact with the customer and may provide a number of services including choice of product, credit facilities and delivery.

As we saw above, some retailers are taking on tasks that have traditionally been performed by other channel intermediaries. Changes in how retailers operate have largely been brought about by the increasing power of the large supermarket chains. As the chains have grown, smaller, independent retailers have gone, unable to compete on either price, marketing expertise or spending power.

These changes have occurred not just because of the supermarket companies' expertise. Other factors such as increased car ownership, increased ownership of freezers, both husband and wife working (meaning shopping is done in the evening or at weekends, rather than during the day in the high street), and the demand for one-stop shopping. Thus shopping trips are less frequent, but more can be purchased on each trip and stored in safe conditions by the consumer.

## Activity 1

Explain how a company of your choice 'places' its products in front of Consumers (i.e. what channels of distribution are used)?

## 6.3  Choice of channel

It may not be the case that a shorter channel is preferable to a longer one. The choice of channel depends on the product and the target market.

A shorter channel favours larger and expensive products that are not purchased very often, products requiring a high level of after-sales service, and products where the consumers are concentrated in distinct geographic areas.

Longer channels are acceptable when the target market is large and spread out, when a low price is more important than a high level of service, and when the product is purchased frequently.

Obviously there is no point in adding intermediaries if they are not needed, and if they do not perform a useful function and make the whole operation more efficient and effective.

If a company wants its goods to be available to all and sundry, it will seek to use as many intermediaries as possible, to give wide geographic and social coverage. However, a valid marketing decision may be made to restrict the outlets at which a certain product is available, for example, expensive scents or upmarket cars. This will require few outlets and thus fewer intermediaries.

It is called 'intensive' distribution when the products are made as widely available as possible. Typical examples are newspapers, razor blades or ladies' hosiery. Such products are typically inexpensive and purchased frequently.

For more expensive items and items that are purchased only rarely, a form of distribution known as 'selective' or 'exclusive' is preferred. In selective distribution, only selected outlets are chosen to carry particular products. For example, certain manufacturers of ladies' fashion items only allow them to be sold in certain department stores. Exclusive distribution is a more extreme form of this, and may allow only one outlet within a geographic region to stock a product, for example, a Rolls Royce dealership.

## Activity 2

List products that are distributed intensively, selectively and exclusively.

Other factors that affect the choice of channel include how much control the manufacturer wishes to exert (as shorter channels allow greater control), the degree of flexibility that is required (i.e. how quickly can changes be made to the method of distribution, can the volumes be increased easily), and the cost effectiveness of the different channels (agents should be cheaper than a full-time salesforce, but there is less control over them).

In addition, the requirements of customer service need to be considered, and decisions made as to whether servicing is performed by the manufacturer's direct employees or by another member of the channel.

Like all marketing decisions, the choice of channel must be based on consumer needs and on the company's strategic objectives.

## Activity 3

What type of channel intermediaries (including retail outlet) would be chosen by manufacturers of the following

a) tinned soup

b) designer dresses

c) refrigerators.

## 6.4 Summary

In this chapter we have considered the methods of distribution open to a company, and in particular channel intermediaries and the choice of channel.

Intermediaries increase the efficiency of the distribution system and act to the benefit of both consumers and producers. A typical channel intermediary may be a wholesaler, an agent or a retailer.

The type of product affects the choice of channel, and in particular the length of the channel. A company's overall marketing strategy also is of great importance when selecting a channel. The channel chosen must fit within this strategy.

## Further reading

G Lancaster and L Massingham, *Essentials of Marketing*, McGraw-Hill, London, 2nd edn, 1993, Chapter 10.

M J Baker (ed.), *The Marketing Book*, Butterworth-Heinemann, 2nd edn, 1991, Chapter 20 (M Christopher)

CIM Study Text, Certificate, *Marketing Fundamentals*, BPP Publishing Ltd, London 1994, Chapter 7.

P Kotler, *Marketing Management*, Prentice-Hall, Englewood Cliffs, 7th edn, 1991, Chapters 19 and 20.

## Exercises

### Progress questions

*These questions are designed to help you to remember the key points in this chapter. The answers are given on page 91.*

1   The major advantage of using channel intermediaries is ...................................................

   ..................................................................................................................................................

2   Agents are extensively used in ..........................................................................................

3   The role of wholesalers is changing because ....................................................................

4   A large number of channel intermediaries will mean that the product is ..................

   ..................................................................................................................................................

### Review questions

*These questions will help you to check your understanding of the key concepts in this chapter. Other sources (e.g. from the further reading list) will help you to give a fuller answer. The appropriate section of this chapter is noted at the end of each section.*

5   How do channel intermediaries produce efficiencies for both producers and consumers? (Section 6.2.1)

6   Who are the three main channel intermediaries and what are their roles? (Section 6.2.2)

7   What factors cause a shorter channel to be chosen rather than a longer one?

*Multiple choice questions*

8　Which of the following is *not* a channel intermediary:
   a)　wholesaler
   b)　retailer
   c)　commission agent
   d)　service engineer

9　Which of the following products is distributed selectively:
   a)　Barbie dolls
   b)　Antler luggage
   c)　McVitie's digestives
   d)　*The Daily Telegraph*

10　Which of the following would *not* favour a short channel of distribution:
   a)　sausages
   b)　perfume
   c)　scotch whiskey
   d)　hardback novels

*Practice questions*

11　Using examples, explain the advantages of using a restricted number and type of outlet for certain products.

12　When and why might a company decide to use an agent for its exporting activities?

13　Using examples, outline one long and one short channel of distribution.

*Questions for advanced students*

14　How important is the retail outlet (your answer should consider different types of stores – chain, franchised (e.g. The Body Shop), department and individual – their consumer-friendliness, and their similarities and differences)?

15　What advantages does greater control over the channel of distribution give to the large supermarket chains?

16　Explain how Place integrates with the other elements of the marketing mix.

## Assignment

Franchising has become increasingly popular over the last ten years. Write a short report explaining what franchising is and why the number of franchises has increased.

# 7 *Marketing research*

## 7.1 Introduction

Information is the lifeblood of all companies, whatever market sector they operate in. Information is needed to inform decision makers, to direct the sales team, to ensure the right production levels are set, and to know what customers want.

All too often, however, the collection and management of information is ignored or handled haphazardly. Managers do not know where to find information, or they are provided with too much information that is irrelevant to their problem, or the information arrives too late, or the information is incomplete. This applies to marketing-related information as much as to other types, and indeed the changes that have been taking place over the last decade have only served to increase the need for accurate and up-to-date marketing information.

These changes include:

a) The rise in international or global marketing – as companies start operating outside their old 'home' territories they need more information about the new markets they are entering.

b) Changing buyer attitudes – consumers are changing, they are less faithful to brands, and as needs become satisfied the consumer's wants take on increasing importance.

c) Competition is becoming more complicated – once only price mattered, but as products become more differentiated and segmentised, companies need information on the effectiveness of their marketing mix.

These changes have increased the need for companies, and especially companies that consider themselves to be market-oriented, to gather more information. This information will be about all aspects of the company's activities, but in particular about the market in which it operates, about its customers, and about its customers' perceptions of and belief in the company and the goods or services it offers.

Thus information will be sought about PEST (political, economic, social and technological) factors affecting the market. Existing customers will be 'examined' to see, for example, how alike they are or why they buy a particular product. And companies will try to discover what the market and consumers think about them, what they are doing right or wrong, if their advertising is successful in reaching its objectives, and if their products are fulfilling the market's needs.

This deluge of information has made it essential for every company to have a 'Marketing Information System' (MIS). Kotler, in his book *Marketing Management*, defined an MIS as "consisting of people, equipment and procedures to gather, sort, analyse, evaluate and distribute needed, timely and accurate information to marketing decision makers". Without the right information, decisions are made in the dark and become little more than guesswork. However, by getting the necessary facts, figures and opinions, it is possible to make decisions that are based on reality and have a chance of turning out to be good decisions.

Sources of marketing information can be found inside companies and include order-despatch-invoice records and sales reports. They also include information available from trade journals, conferences and exhibitions.

Other marketing information can only be obtained by actually looking for it. It is this area of active marketing research on which the remainder of this chapter will concentrate. By the end of this chapter, the student should

❐ understand the need for marketing research

❐ know to which marketing activities research can be applied

❐ understand the marketing research process

❐ know the difference between primary and secondary data

❐ understand the concept of test marketing.

## 7.2 Types of marketing research

Marketing research can be applied to all four of the marketing variables (the four Ps) and also to sales and 'the market'.

### 7.2.1 Product research

Product research is an essential component of new product development and it is used in the following ways:

a) Concept testing

As we saw in the section of Chapter 2 on new product development, once a new product idea has been generated, and has passed through the screening process, it is necessary to test the concept, or idea, of the new product. This often involves selecting groups of the supposed users/consumers of the product, describing the product to them, and then quizzing them on their likely purchase intentions. The answers that are received should then dictate if the product development process moves forward to the next step.

b) Prototype testing

If a new product proposal gets past the concept stage and prototypes are produced, it is necessary to test consumer reaction to the product. Again groups of likely consumers are shown the product (and asked to use it or taste it, as appropriate) and asked if they would buy it and their wider opinions of the prototype. At this stage changes can be made relatively cheaply. For example, the taste can be altered, the size can be changed, or the mode of operation can be adjusted.

Packaging will also be tested. For example, is the colour acceptable to the target market and does that market regard it as being 'right' for the product, is it easy to open, does it convey enough information, and is it a convenient size for the product?

The third stage of new product development testing, test marketing, will be discussed more fully later in this chapter.

## Activity 1

What type of people would ideally make up a test panel for
a)  a new industrial cleansing agent
b)  a new type of disposable nappy
c)  a new car polish

### 7.2.2  Pricing research

Although consumers are influenced by more than the price of the product, many companies will adjust their prices until they find the price that gives the best return in terms of production and sales costs versus sales income. A lower price may give better sales and lower unit cost of production (economies of scale), but the profit may not meet the company's requirements. Equally a higher price may increase the income per item, but sales may be too low to sustain production costs.

Unfortunately, and certainly with new products, it is very difficult to quantify the level of sales for a given price. Thus a certain amount of price research is inevitable.

### 7.2.3  Promotion research

This covers areas such as media selection, copy testing and campaign effectiveness.

a)  Media selection

It is essential to collect as much data as possible on possible media for an advertising campaign before starting the campaign. The information should include: audience size (i.e. the number of people who will see the advertisement in that media), the number of times the audience will see it, how many of the total audience exposed to the advertisement are members of the real target audience, and the cost per target audience member.

b)  Copy testing

There are some sophisticated physiological ways of testing the effectiveness of advertisements, including tracking eye movements and measuring heart rate. Small groups of possible consumers are also set up and asked for their opinions of advertising or promotional material.

c)  Campaign effectiveness

This is concerned with measuring how sales (or some other indicator) changes from the start to the finish of a campaign. As we saw in Chapter 3 on Promotion, all campaigns should have an objective, and this type of research is concerned with measuring if that objective has been reached.

## Activity 2

How might a company promoting a new brand of toothpaste measure the effectiveness of a campaign to get people to try the toothpaste?

### 7.2.4 Place research

This includes such activities as

a) collecting information on customer location to help to decide the location of warehouse and distribution centres, and

b) gathering data to be used when deciding where to open retail outlets.

Such data would include the socio-economic characteristics of the neighbourhood, competitors, other shops, ease of parking, and other amenities. Every High Street has a 'good' side and a 'bad' side.

### 7.2.5 Sales and market research

This area of marketing research includes:

a) measuring or estimating the size of the market

b) identifying market trends (and the reasons behind them)

c) sales forecasting

d) competitor information and activity

e) market share.

These are some of the most common areas for marketing research and form the basis of many corporate decisions. It is looked at in more detail in the remainder of this chapter.

## 7.3 In-house or specialist agency

The first question to be asked when contemplating marketing research is 'who is to do it?'. Can the work be done by an in-house team or is it necessary to call on the expertise of outside specialists?

Obviously not all companies have the personnel with sufficient time available, or the right skills, to undertake marketing research. However, an in-house marketing research department should be faster and have a greater knowledge of the company's products and the markets in which it is operating.

An outside agency has the advantage that the staff are likely to be competent in a range of research specialties and will have a broad knowledge of many different markets.

An outside agency may also produce research that is more objective, as it is more likely to report the discovered facts rather than try to make the facts fit the company's hopes or desires (especially if there is internal pressure to come to a particular conclusion).

It is likely that the larger the company, the more likely it is to have an in-house marketing research department, while smaller companies will need to call upon the services of specialised marketing research organisations. It should be noted that such organisations exist across the whole range of industrial and consumer sectors.

## 7.4  The marketing research process

Marketing research should only be undertaken if the results will help to understand a problem better, and thus lead to a solution of that problem. It should also be borne in mind that the value of the information obtained (or rather the consequences of having the information) should be greater than the cost of the research.

If after consideration of these two questions it is decided to go ahead with the research, then the research process can start. This is split into five distinct phases:

i)   defining the problem and thus setting the objectives of the research

ii)   producing a research plan

iii)  collecting the information

iv)  analysing the information

v)   reporting the results.

These phases will now be looked at in a little more detail.

### 7.4.1  Defining the problem and setting the objectives

Only if the problem is properly defined and the objectives of the research clearly agreed, will the research process bring the information needed to solve the problem. The definition must focus on the problem, but must be broad enough to allow unexpected answers to appear.

For example, the manager of a foundry might say "I'm thinking of investing in some new moulding plant, but I need to know if I can sell enough castings to my customers to justify it". Market research is not really needed to answer this question, as the sales team should be able to supply the answer as to whether existing customers will increase their orders. However, market research will be needed to find out about other market segments and the customers in those segments. However, the problem must be defined in such a way so that only those segments whose demand in terms of piece size and order volume are suitable to the new moulding plant are investigated.

In this example the objectives will be to identify segments that could be supplied, to discover current purchase levels, to learn about trends within the sectors, and to find out as much as possible about possible customers and competitors.

Whether using an in-house department or an outside agency, the manager of the research team should always prepare a brief defining the problem and listing the objectives. This must then be agreed with the client. The brief should also outline the research plan.

### Activity 3

What is the market research problem, and thus the objectives, for somebody thinking of setting up a fast-response printing service.

### 7.4.2  The research plan

When the problem has been defined and the objectives have been agreed, it is possible to formulate a research plan. This will outline the data collection methods to be used.

In essence there are two ways of collecting data: from secondary sources and from primary sources.

Secondary data sources consist of data that has already been collected and 'published' in some way. 'Internal' sources include customer records, sales records, invoices and previous research reports. 'External' sources are numerous and the following are just a few examples of easily available information sources:

❏ Business Monitors, published by HMSO, including Production, Service and Distribution, and Miscellaneous Series. These cover production, sales, imports and exports, employment levels, and a variety of other categorisations, depending on the business.

❏ Census of Population, collected every 10 years and containing a lot of information about the population of the UK.

❏ Trade and Technical Associations. These bodies are often extremely knowledgeable about their particular areas, and are able to provide a lot of useful information.

❏ Directories and Magazines/Journals of specific trades or industry sectors.

❏ Market surveys published by e.g. *The Economist* or *The Financial Times*.

This list is by no means complete, but should at least show that there are many sources of secondary data.

## Activity 4

List some sources of secondary data that would be of interest to a company manufacturing and selling microwave ovens.

It is unlikely that secondary data will supply all the answers, but it is a useful starting point, and may well show from where the primary data should be collected.

Primary data is defined as data that is collected for a particular purpose, not having been collected previously. It will be focused on the previously defined problem and objectives. There are four possible information collection methods: surveys, group interviews, observation, and experimentation.

The most common method is by surveys using prepared questionnaires. Questionnaire design is a large subject in its own right, but it is worth considering a few points here. When designing a questionnaire it is important to consider how the answers will be analysed. Is the information sought solely quantitative (yes/no, preference from 1 to 10) or is there a qualitative element? Questions can be open, requiring a reasoned response, they can be closed requiring a yes/no response or a multiple choice response, or they can seek to find the respondent's attitude to something (for example ranging from 'like a lot' to 'dislike a lot'). Questionnaires can be mailed to respondents, the respondents can be telephoned, or the respondents can be questioned face to face. Mailing is cheapest, but the response will be low and it is not possible to ask follow-up questions. Ways of increasing the response include freepost replies and incentives for those replying (for example entry into a prize draw and money-off offers).

Telephoning is likely to be the quickest method, but the respondent may not have the information to hand and indeed the ideal respondent may not be available.

Personal, face-to-face interviews are likely to elicit the greatest amount of information but they can be expensive and very time consuming.

A major problem encountered during all collection of primary data is the sample used. In most cases it will be impossible (in financial if not in logistical terms) to contact all of a target market. It is therefore necessary to select a representative sample. This can be done on the basis of a random or systematic choice from the market of interest, by selecting special characteristics of some within the market and choosing all or some of them as the sample, or by choosing a particular geographic area and choosing the sample from within it.

Whatever method is chosen, it is generally agreed that the larger the sample size, the greater will be the accuracy of the results.

Group interviews, when 6–10 people gather in a group with a trained and knowledgeable interviewer, are often used prior to carrying out a larger survey as they will give an idea of consumer attitudes. They are also used during concept and prototype testing phases of new product development.

As the name implies, observational research requires consumers, retail outlets, competitors etc. to be watched. It might be used when deciding on the location of a retail outlet, for example how many people go past a particular point in the high street; visiting an exhibition to see competitors' products; using competitors' services to compare them with yours.

Finally experimentation involves changing one variable while keeping the others constant to see what the effect is (usually on sales). Thus price can be altered to see if the level of sales changes. Packaging can be altered for the same reason. Different advertising can be used in different regions of the country.

In conclusion, depending on the problem, a plan is drawn up to collect the necessary data.

### 7.4.3  Collecting the information

If the plan is good, then this stage of the process should be straightforward, but it may not be easy. For example, when conducting surveys it may not be easy to contact the right number of respondents, and the respondents who are contacted may give biased answers. The only thing that can be done is to keep going until enough respondents have been contacted and enough answers have been obtained.

### 7.4.4  Analysing the information

Depending on the information being gathered, this may involve complicated mathematical procedures (usually done with the aim of computers) or objective analysis of qualitative responses.

### 7.4.5  Reporting the results

The Research Report should report the facts, and not the researcher's prejudices. It should outline (as appropriate) the research methods used, data sources, sampling techniques, the questionnaire used, data collection methods, and the analysis methods. The findings should be set out clearly, and lengthy lists of data or mathematical analysis should be relegated to appendices. Always remember that the research was carried out as the result of a problem and the report should provide the answer to the problem.

## 7.5 Test marketing

Test Marketing is the process whereby a product is placed on sale in a selected area only. The purpose is to measure the reactions of consumers to the product, the promotional methods being used, the packaging and the price. In addition, the method of distribution will be studied and retailers will be asked for their thoughts about the product.

Test Marketing will give an indication not only of likely sales when the product is sold nationally or internationally but will also allow the company and its marketing department to gauge the effectiveness of the different elements of the marketing mix. It is, of course, necessary to set objectives for the test market so that the success or otherwise of the operation can be judged.

The test area selected should, as far as possible, be a microcosm of the total market. It must be large enough to be representative of the whole market for the product, yet small enough to allow detailed research at a reasonable cost. Usually, several areas will be selected for testing a new product, which also gives the advantage of being able to alter aspects of the marketing mix from area to area.

A potential drawback of Test Marketing is that it can give competitors advance notice of your new products, and thus in some cases allow them to launch a similar product to the whole market before you have even finished the test marketing. However, the advantage of being able to fine tune a marketing plan before a national launch is extremely valuable. Problems can be identified and solved, the promotional campaign can be launched in the knowledge that it works and retailers can be assured that the product will be successful. (Conversely, if the test marketing produces very few sales, then the company can be saved from the high costs of a national launch followed by the embarrassment of a public failure.)

### Activity 5

Where, in general terms, might you choose to test market

a) a new brand of disposable nappy

b) a new breakfast cereal

c) a new lager

## 7.6 Summary

This chapter has looked at the basis of marketing research. We have seen how it can be applied to all four elements of the marketing mix.

We have also seen how research can be applied to a 'market', and the process whereby information on the market is gathered. This involves defining the problem and objectives, producing a plan, collecting information, analysing the information, and reporting the results.

Finally we looked briefly at test marketing, a necessary activity that is full of pitfalls.

## Further reading

P Kotler, *Marketing Management*, Prentice-Hall, Englewood Cliffs, 7th edn, 1991, Chapters 4 and 9.

G Lancaster and L Massingham, *Essentials of Marketing*, McGraw-Hill, London, 2nd edn, 1993, Chapters 5 and 6.

CIM Study Text, Certificate, *Marketing Fundamentals*, BPP Publishing, London, 1994, Chapter 4.

## Exercises

*Progress questions*

*These questions are designed to help you to remember the key points in this chapter. The answers are given on page 91.*

Complete the following sentences:

1    Product research is part of ........................................................................................

2    The three areas of promotion research are ............................................................

3    The advantages of using an outside market research agency are ........................

.............................................................................................................................................

4    The first phase of market research is to ................................................................

5    The two types of market research data are ...........................................................

6    Test marketing is .....................................................................................................

Select the correct response to the following statements.

7    Attitudes of consumers are changing.

True ☐ False ☐

8    Prototype testing is not necessary if the concept of a new product is accepted by senior management.

True ☐ False ☐

9    It does not matter on which side of the High Street your shop is located.

True ☐ False ☐

10   Market research should always be conducted by outside agencies.

True ☐ False ☐

11   Secondary data will usually provide all the answers.

True ☐ False ☐

*Review questions*

*These questions will help you to check your understanding of the key concepts in this chapter. Other sources (e.g. from the Further Reading list) will help you to give a fuller answer. The appropriate section of this chapter is noted at the end of each question.*

12  Describe some of the changes that have been taking place in the marketing environment. (Section 7.1)

13  How is marketing research used in new product development? (Section 7.2.1)

14  How is marketing research related to promotion? (Section 7.2.3)

15  What are the disadvantages of undertaking market research in-house? (Section 7.3)

16  How, before starting the research process, does defining the problem help to set objectives (use examples)? (Section 7.4.1)

17  What is the difference between primary and secondary data? (Section 7.4.2)

18  Why is test marketing important? (Section 7.5)

*Multiple choice questions*

19  Which of the following would not be a sensible subject for marketing research:
    a)  the colour of packaging
    b)  the remuneration of the salesforce
    c)  the effectiveness of proposed advertisements
    d)  the best location for a retail outlet.

20  Which of the following is not a source of secondary data:
    a)  trade journals
    b)  a retailer stocking your product
    c)  government statistics
    d)  customer sales records.

21  Which of the following should always be found in a marketing information system:
    a)  a filing cabinet
    b)  a computer database
    c)  a marketing information system manager
    d)  a procedure for gathering and analysing information.

*Practice questions*

22  Why is it important for all companies concerned with marketing to have a 'Marketing Information System'?

23  Explain how market research contributes to choosing the media for a promotional campaign.

24 Discuss the advantages of the three most common ways of researching using questionnaires (postal, telephone or face-to-face).

## Assignment

You are the project manager in a market research agency. Your client has identified a way of improving the wear-resistance (and thus the lifetime) of components used in mining machinery (the machinery used to turn the rock cut from the ground into the precious metal and the waste stone). The components usually last 3–4 weeks, but with improved wear-resistance they could last 8–12 weeks.

Your client needs to know (a) if the mining companies would be interested and (b) the likely size of the market.

Required

Prepare an outline research plan. This should include possible sources of secondary data, what sort of primary data you would want to collect, and how you would collect the data.

Any assumptions you make should be listed as such.

# 8 *Marketing management*

## 8.1 Introduction

This final chapter is concerned with marketing management in terms of setting objectives, selection of marketing strategy and managing the marketing mix to implement the strategy and achieve the objectives.

The preceding chapters in this book have looked at the individual elements of the marketing mix (product, promotion, price and place) and have outlined their characteristics. The inter-relationship between them has been emphasised and aspects of their management have been discussed. It is now necessary to set them in the wider context of corporate objectives.

On completing this chapter, the student should:

❏ understand what is meant by the corporate mission

❏ be able to carry out a SWOT analysis

❏ understand the need for corporate objectives and how to set them

❏ understand the basis of strategy selection

❏ know the contents of a marketing plan.

## 8.2 The mission statement

It has become increasingly common over the last 10–15 years for companies, of all sizes and serving many different markets, to have a 'mission statement'. This is a statement that defines the business, and should be couched in terms of the customers, their needs, and how those needs are met.

It is important to focus on the customer's needs, rather than what the company provides. This way 'marketing myopia', defined by Levitt in the early 1960s, will be avoided. The most oft-quoted example given by Levitt was the American railway industries. The companies involved had all believed that they were in the business of providing a railway service. What they were in fact doing was providing a transportation service for their customers. If they had realised that their mission was to fulfil their customers' needs, rather than to run a railway system, they would have been able to take advantage of the technological advances (especially air travel) and continue to provide a transportation service for their customers.

Thus a mission statement must be focused on the needs of the customer, and should express what those needs are. Thus a company providing a dry cleaning service is fulfilling a need for clean clothes. A company supplying baked beans is fulfilling a need for a cheap, convenient and reasonably nutritious food.

The customer group or groups to be served must be expressed. Baked beans may be supplied to those on a limited budget or to people wanting to prepare light meals quickly. The company will decide which of these market segments it is serving and adapt its marketing mix appropriately.

Finally the mission statement will explain how the customers' needs are met. In the case of baked beans this could be by using the lowest cost raw ingredients thus giving a low priced product that is widely available. In the case of dry cleaning, it could be by operating dry cleaning shops in selected areas and offering a 24 hour service.

## Activity 1

Does your company or college have a mission statement? If so, what is it? Does it identify the customers, their needs, and how these needs are met? How could the mission statement be improved?

If your company or college does not have a mission statement, what should it be?

## 8.3 SWOT analysis

The corporate mission statement sets out in very broad terms the reason for the business to exist. It is then necessary to see how well the company will be able to carry out its mission. This is done by assessing both the internal resources and the external environment.

The assessment is commonly called a SWOT analysis, which stands for Strengths, Weaknesses, Opportunities and Threats. Strengths and weaknesses refer to the company (internal), while opportunities and threats refer to the external environment and the market.

### 8.3.1 Strengths and weaknesses

Strengths and weaknesses should be assessed over the whole company, and would normally cover:

> financial standing
>
> physical attributes (e.g. buildings)
>
> personnel
>
> distribution
>
> marketing
>
> research and development
>
> manufacturing.

This list will vary from company to company, and the importance of different elements will vary depending on the type of business.

It is important to assess the level of the strength or weakness and also to assess them in comparison with major competitors. If all competitors are weak in a certain area, then our own weakness in that area is less important, but if they have strengths where we have weaknesses, then remedial action is needed. Equally, if we have strengths where they have weaknesses, this may show an area where competitive advantage can be gained.

### 8.3.2 Opportunities and threats

Opportunities and threats relate to both the markets in which the company operates and the whole environment within which the company and its markets are situated.

Opportunities and threats are related to the PEST (political, economic, social, technological) factors considered in Chapter 1. They may be long term or short term in nature and impact.

Opportunities and threats will affect all companies operating in a particular market, but what may be a threat to one company may be an opportunity to another. It is usual to try to relate the opportunities and threats presented to the company with its strengths and weaknesses. This enables the company to decide if an external factor can be exploited, through its strengths, as an opportunity, or if, because of weaknesses, it should be guarded against as a threat.

Figures 8.1 and 8.2 show opportunity and threat matrices (from Kotler, Marketing Management), which are a way of classifying the action needed in the face of threats and opportunities.

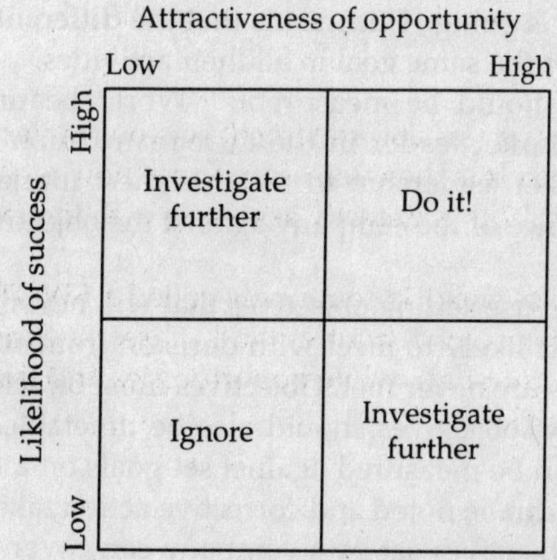

Attractiveness of opportunity

|  | Low | High |
|---|---|---|
| **High** | Investigate further | Do it! |
| **Low** | Ignore | Investigate further |

*(Likelihood of success)*

*Figure 8.1  Opportunity matrix*

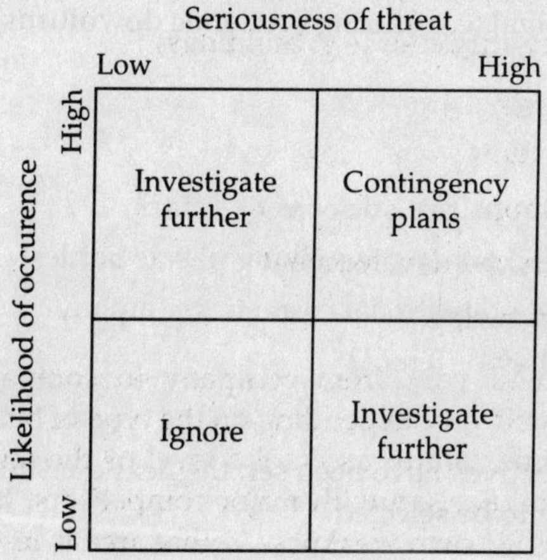

Seriousness of threat

|  | Low | High |
|---|---|---|
| **High** | Investigate further | Contingency plans |
| **Low** | Ignore | Investigate further |

*(Likelihood of occurence)*

*Figure 8.2  Threat matrix*

For a company to be able to carry out a meaningful analysis of the environment in which it operates it needs to keep up to date with what is going on in that environment. This should be in terms of intelligence about the markets it is serving as well as wider ranging knowledge of PEST factors.

*Activity 2*

Carry out a SWOT analysis for your company or college. How well do your strengths and weaknesses allow you to face the opportunities and threats you have identified?

## 8.4 Marketing objectives

We discussed in Chapter 3 the need for objectives for promotional campaigns. Much the same applies to a company's corporate objectives.

The objectives must be specific, so that everyone in the company knows where the company is going. This means that the different departments in a company will all be aiming for the same goal in all their activities.

They should be measurable. 'World beating' sounds good but does not mean much. 'Market leader in the European Union' does mean something (assuming we take market leadership to mean highest market share). It is only by measuring the performance of the company against the objective that it is possible to tell if it has been achieved.

It is no use setting objectives that will never be met. This becomes a pointless exercise and is likely to meet with derision from staff. It will also cause demoralisation if objectives are never met. Objectives must be achievable and relevant.

Finally, objectives should also be timetabled again so that the company's performance can be measured against set goals on a timetable. This way failure to meet the set goals can be noted and corrective action taken.

The objectives set by a company can cover a wide variety of goals, and there will commonly be several (hopefully compatible) objectives. It is likely that one objective will be to achieve a certain level of profitability, possibly related to sales turnover. Other objectives may cover market share, expansion, technical leadership and innovation, survival (e.g. during economic downturns), internationalisation.

*Activity 3*

What would be realistic objectives for

a) a small company supplying plastic bottles

b) a large international cosmetics company?

Why are they different?

Once objectives have been set, the next question is how to achieve them. This requires a strategy to be selected.

## 8.5 Strategy selection

An introductory text such as this can only deal superficially with marketing strategy decisions. However, it is worth noting at this stage the difference between objectives, strategy and tactics. In simple terms, objectives set the goal, strategy outlines broadly how the goal will be reached, and tactics detail how the strategy will be implemented.

What we are concerned with here is how the strategy is selected (in essence, Chapters 2–6 dealt with tactics).

### 8.5.1 The Ansoff Matrix

One of the most popular ways of looking at the different strategies available to a company is the 'Ansoff Matrix', illustrated in Figure 8.3. The four boxes within the matrix represent alternative strategies.

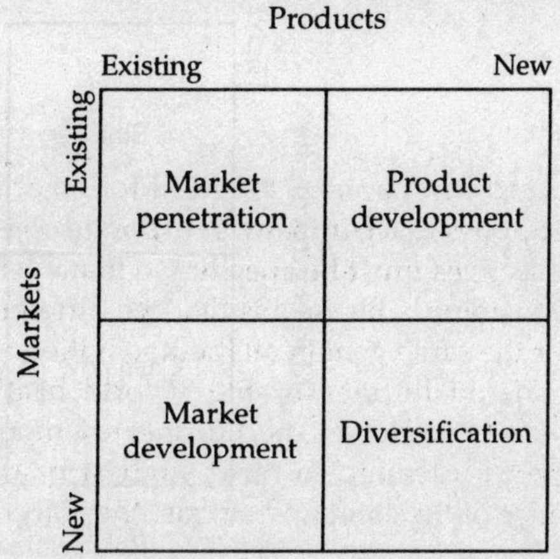

*Figure 8.3 Ansoff matrix*

#### Market penetration

Increasing sales of existing products within existing markets. During the 'growth' period of a market this can be achieved by growing with the market, but in a mature market increased sales can only be achieved by taking market share from competitors (with implications regarding price wars).

#### Market development

Selling existing products to new markets, for example, overseas (i.e. exporting) or a different market segment.

#### Product development

Producing new products for sale in existing markets, for example, a new shampoo from a cosmetics company.

#### Diversification

Producing new products for new markets. This is a high risk strategy as it assumes that the company has experience of neither the new product ranges nor the new markets it will enter.

There are other methods of strategy selection based on concepts such as market growth and relative market share (the Boston Consulting Group Matrix or Boston Box) or market attractiveness and competitive position (the McKinsey/General Electric Matrix). These are also known as 'Portfolio Analysis', and will now be briefly explained.

### 8.5.2   The BCG Matrix

The BCG Matrix is illustrated in Figure 8.4. The horizontal axis shows market share relative to the market leader, whilst the vertical axis shows the rate of growth of the market.

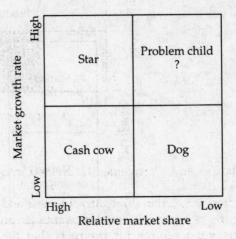

*Figure 8.4  BCG matrix*

The matrix is divided into four boxes. The top right is for 'Question Marks' (also known as 'Problem Children'). These are products that although in a rapidly growing market only command a relatively small market share. Products in this category frequently require large promotional expenditure, with the aim of moving them into the 'Stars' category.

'Stars' are the products every company likes to have – products with a large market share in a rapidly growing market. Expenditure will be needed to keep them in this category, but given their position as leaders in an expanding market, they should repay that expenditure many times over.

However, stars may fade, and when a market reaches maturity, and the rate of growth declines, market leaders can enter the category of 'Cash Cow'. This is the term used for products that, because of the stability of the market, generate income for a company without being too large a drain on resources.

The final category of product is a 'Dog'. This is the term for a product with a small market share in a market with low growth. The decision to be made about such products is whether to get out of the market (shoot the dog) or try to turn the dog into a cash cow. This last option is likely to be very expensive and so is rarely followed.

Thus the BCG Matrix is a useful tool for categorising products. It can help strategy selection by allowing products to be seen, in a schematic way, as belonging to a particular set, and so strategies appropriate to that set can be applied.

### 8.5.3   McKinsey/General Electric Matrix

The McKinsey/General Electric Matrix is illustrated in Figure 8.5, and shows the relationship between the attractiveness of a market and the company's competitive position (or competence) within that market.

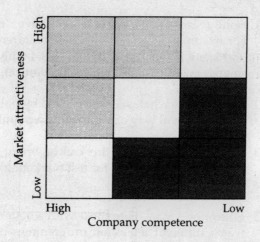

*Figure 8.5 McKinsey/General Electric matrix*

The Matrix can be conveniently divided into three regions: invest, investigate and ignore.

The top left section (high attractiveness and high competence), shown light grey in the figure, is where a company wants its products to be. This represents markets showing good returns for products that the company is good at producing and marketing. This is the area where the company should invest.

The middle section, shown white in the figure, is to be investigated. The top right is for an attractive market with low competence where the investigation is centred on whether the company can improve its competence, and so move products in this area to the left (i.e. to high attractiveness and high competence). The middle box represents medium attractiveness and medium competence, and so investigations will centre on whether either or both can be improved. The bottom left box represents an unattractive market that the company is very competent at serving. It could be a declining market where the company was once market leader. In this case the investigation should centre on whether the market is as unattractive as it seems.

The bottom right hand section of the matrix (low attractiveness and low competence), coloured dark grey in the figure, is where a company does not want to be. If a market is not attractive and moreover the company is not good at serving this market, then to carry on or to start marketing products in these areas will be a waste of resources.

### 8.5.4 Market segmentation

The final area of strategy selection to be looked at is market segmentation. This concept is fundamental to good marketing practice, and is the process of dividing a market into manageable 'segments' using a variety of criteria.

a) Consumer segmentation

   ❑ Age – the age of the consumer will often dictate their purchasing habits, their reading habits and their television watching habits. Many products are aimed at a particular age group.

   ❑ Sex – obviously some products are for women and some for men, but this can extend further to items such as cars, some of which are thought of as more feminine than others.

❏ Family size – larger families will have different needs from smaller families. For example, a family with four children will buy a giant size tin of baked beans or a larger family car, while a family with only one child will purchase a smaller quantity of beans and could manage with a smaller car.

❏ Social class – whatever may be said by politicians to the contrary, social class is still a powerful way of segmenting a population.

❏ Geographic location – this can be broad-based, for example an independent television area (such as for test marketing), or by type of housing or residential neighbourhood.

❏ Education – very often those with a better formal education will be inclined to watch different television programmes or read different magazines to those who left school at 16 with no qualifications.

❏ Lifestyle – segmentation by lifestyle is usually based on the target group's activities (leisure, work, hobbies etc.), interests (home, job, reading etc.) and opinions (politics, social issues, culture etc.). This type of segmentation is becoming increasingly popular and important, and is often informed by long questionnaires sent to households around the country.

b) Industrial segmentation

❏ Size of company – very often large and small firms will have very different buying procedures, these being very formalised in large companies.

❏ Type of industry – although a product may be used in several different industries, the marketing approach may need to be different to reflect, for example, the different trade media available, the different typical order size, or the different organisation types.

❏ Geographic location – this can be on an international scale, for example, European Union, North America, South East Asia, or on a national basis such as South East England, Wales, the Midlands.

For a segment to be exploited, it is necessary that it can be identified and its size measured, there must be effective ways of promoting the product to those making up the segment, and it must offer sufficient return to match the company's objectives.

However, segmentation has the advantage of allowing a company to take a 'rifle shot' rather than 'blunderbuss' approach to its marketing. Products and promotion can be made to appeal to the segment under consideration, and altered as necessary for other segments. This benefits both the consumer and the producer.

*Activity 4*

List some products that are segmented by:

age

sex

social class

type of industry.

## 8.6 Marketing planning

Once the objectives have been set and the strategy chosen, it is necessary to formulate a plan to implement the strategy and detail the tactics to be used.

The following outlines the contents of a marketing plan. The contents will, of course, vary depending on the company, its products, its market position, its objectives, and the chosen strategy. This outline can be taken as a good guide for those new to this subject.

The first steps are to analyse the current situation.

a)  Mission statement

This is needed to ensure that the plan is devised, read and implemented with the company's mission in mind.

b)  Market analysis

Data on the target market(s) – size, growth potential, customer needs and buying behaviour, market segmentation.

c)  Competitor analysis

Description of major competitors, including size, goals (if known), financial standing, market share, product portfolio, marketing strategies, capabilities.

d)  Marketing mix analysis

Information on product lines, sales, profit margins; pricing policy; effectiveness of previous promotional strategy and tactics; factors affecting distribution and the most effective distribution channels.

e)  Environmental analysis

Social, legal, economic, political and technological factors affecting the market.

f)  SWOT analysis

Based largely on (b), (c), (d) and (e), a series of simple statements, ranked in order of importance, outlining the major internal strengths and weaknesses of the company and the external opportunities and threats facing the company.

At this point the first stage of marketing planning, analysis of the current situation, has been completed. The next stage is to set objectives.

g)  Setting objectives

First financial objectives will be set, for example, rate of return on investment of 15% for the next three years, next profits of £x million in the year after. Secondly, the financial objectives will be converted into marketing objectives. This will include unit sales levels, at specified prices, in each market, target market share, awareness levels. All these objectives should be quantified and time-tabled.

The objectives have now been stated, and it is time to decide how to meet them. This is the strategy that will be adopted, and below the strategy the tactics. In some companies, tactics will be the subject of separate plans generated by the relevant department being guided by the objectives and overall strategy.

h) Markets

Detailing the markets or market segments to be targeted by each product.

i) Positioning statement

A brief statement that sums up the benefits to the consumer of the company's products.

j) Product

For example, new product development, modifications to existing products, added features, quality levels.

k) Price

For example, discounts to retailers, payment terms, skimming or penetration in new markets, policy on price changes, freedom to negotiate prices.

l) Promotion

For example, strategies, tactics and objectives for advertising, public relations, sales promotion and the salesforce.

m) Place

For example, distribution channels to be used, retail outlets to be targeted, delivery systems.

It should be noted that (j), (k), (l) and (m) are what will make or break a marketing plan. The marketing mix, and its interrelationships, is the most important element of a company's marketing activities. It should be noted that it will probably be necessary to produce a separate strategy document for different products and different markets.

Finally, the marketing plan needs to address financial and control matters.

n) Financial return

This should detail forecast sales volumes and income and also production, marketing and selling costs.

o) Controls

This section of the plan outlines how the progress of the plan will be monitored, for example against monthly budget targets and also against the overall corporate objectives and the objectives of the elements of the marketing mix.

p) Contingency plans

The 'what if?' section of the plan. If prior thought has been given to a potential problem, and remedial action planned, then if the problem arises it can be dealt with more efficiently.

If marketing plans are drawn up sensibly and realistically, and they are not then consigned to the bottom drawer, they will be of immense value to a company and its managers.

## 8.7 Summary

This chapter has looked at some aspects of marketing management. In particular, we have seen how a company can assess its present situation (SWOT analysis), set objectives, and select a strategy to reach the objectives. Finally, we have looked briefly at the composition of a marketing plan.

## Further reading

M H B McDonald, *Marketing Plans*, Butterworth-Heinemann, Oxford, 2nd edn, 1989.

G Lancaster & L Massingham, *Essentials of Marketing*, McGraw-Hill, London, 2nd edn, 1993, Chapters 4, 7 and 13.

P Kotler, *Marketing Management*, Prentice-Hall, Englewood Cliffs, 7th edn, 1991, Chapters 3, 10, 14 and 15.

CIM Study Text, Certificate, *Marketing Fundamentals*, BPP Publishing, London, 1994, Chapters 3 and 9.

## Exercises

*Progress questions*

*These questions are designed to help you to remember the key points in this chapter. The answers are given on page 91.*

Complete the following sentences.

1    A SWOT analysis is concerned with ..................................................................

2    A company's objectives must be ....................................................................

3    Market penetration involves ........................................................................

4    Market development involves ........................................................................

5    Product development involves ......................................................................

6    Diversification involves ..............................................................................

## Review questions

*These questions will help you to check your understanding of the key concepts in this chapter. Other sources (e.g. from the Further Reading list) will help you to give a fuller answer. The appropriate section of this chapter is noted at the end of each question.*

7   Why is a mission statement important and what three areas should it address? (Section 8.2)

8   Explain why a SWOT analysis is important. (Section 8.3)

9   Draw an Ansoff matrix. (Section 8.5)

## Multiple choice question

10   Which of the following is not found in a BCG Matrix:
   a)   cash cow
   b)   dog
   c)   dead dodo
   d)   problem child.

## Practice questions

11   Objectives are important, but they must fulfil certain criteria. What are these criteria and why must they be fulfilled?

12   Why is the Ansoff matrix a useful marketing tool?

13   Why is it necessary to have a marketing plan?

14   Explain the reasons for segmenting a market.

### Assignment

You are the Marketing Manager of a company supplying industrial air-conditioning units. The company's objective is to capture 25% of the UK market and 5% of the European market by 2001. The UK market was worth £150m in 1993, and the European market £800m. The size of the air-conditioning units varies, selling from £10,000 to £250,000 depending on the size of the premises. A financial return of 12.5% of turnover is required.

Required

Making such assumptions as are necessary, prepare an outline marketing plan.

You should especially consider market segments, the inter-relationship of the marketing mix, and control measures.

# Answers to progress questions

## Chapter 1

1 Marketing is a management process.
2 The four elements of the marketing mix are product, price, place and promotion.
3 The macro environmental factors to be considered in marketing decisions are political, economic, social and technological.
4 The three ways in which a marketing department can be arranged are by function, by product or by market.
5 False
6 False
7 False
8 True

## Chapter 2

1 The two main types of product classification are consumer goods and industrial goods.
2 More thought is required when buying 'shopping' goods than 'convenience' goods because shopping goods are usually larger purchases.
3 The causes of new product failure include overestimate of market size, the product does not perform as expected, competitive pressures are too strong, the advertising is wrong, and the product is not supported by e.g. retailers.
4 The eight stages of new product development are: idea generation, screening, concept development, marketing strategy, business analysis, product development, test marketing, and commercialisation.
5 The four stages of the product life cycle are introduction, growth, maturity and decline.
6 A penetration pricing policy when introducing a new product involves a low price in order to gain market share.
7 False (specialty goods will not be easily available)
8 False
9 False (being red is a feature)
10 False
11 False
12 False (most are in the mature stage)

## Chapter 3

1 In the marketing communications, the five variables of the communication process are the communicator, the content of the message, the audience, the media and the response.

2  Objectives should be SMART: specific, measurable, achievable, relevant and timetabled.

3  Sales promotion is a useful marketing tool because it is flexible, capable of specific action, not expensive and fast.

4  A problem with 'coupons' as a method of consumer-based sales promotion is that they are often accepted irrespective of whether the presenter of the coupon has purchased the relevant items.

5  The difference between publicity and PR is that publicity just happens when PR is planned and controlled.

6  The media available to a company wishing to advertise are television, radio, cinema, newspapers, magazines and outside.

7  False (the communicator has control through choice of media)

8  False (without objectives, who is to say if it has met the objectives and so been successful)

9  False

10  False

11  False

12  False

*Chapter 4*

1  Personal selling is important because there need be no intermediaries between the producer and the consumer and it allows the consumer's needs to be stressed.

2  Typical information required by a salesman before a sales interview includes the name and position of the person to be seen, previous purchases, the customer's opinion of the salesman's company, and the company's activities and real needs.

3  A trial close of a sale can include asking what colour the buyer would like or when delivery would be convenient.

4  The role of an influencer in a DMU is to provide specialist knowledge or experience.

5  The three ways of organising a salesforce are geographically, by product or by customer type.

6  False

7  False

8  False (the decider may only play a nominal role, with the decision based on the views of the other members of the DMU).

9  False (it depends on the circumstances)

*Chapter 5*

1  Market skimming pricing policy is the name given to the tactic of setting a high price for a new product in order to recoup development costs.

2  Market penetration pricing policy is the name given to the tactic of setting a low price for a new product in order to gain market share.

3  Some typical fixed costs are rates, central overheads, labour costs and promotional costs.

4  Some typical variable costs are raw materials, distribution, packaging and selling costs.

5 In pricing terms, the maturity phase of the product life cycle is characterised by price competition.

6 False

7 False

8 True

9 False

**Chapter 6**

1 The major advantage of using channel intermediaries is that both producers and consumers need to make fewer contacts.

2 Agents are extensively used in exporting.

3 The role of wholesalers is changing because supermarket chains are increasingly acting as their own distributors.

4 A large number of channel intermediaries will mean that the product is widely available.

**Chapter 7**

1 Product research is part of new product development.

2 The three areas of promotion research are media selection, copy testing and campaign effectiveness.

3 The advantages of using an outside market research agency are that its staff will be competent in a range of market research skills.

4 The first phase of market research is to define the problem and thus set objectives.

5 The two types of market research data are primary and secondary.

6 Test marketing is the process by which products are placed on sale in a selected area only.

7 True

8 False

9 False

10 False

11 False

**Chapter 8**

1 A SWOT analysis is concerned with strengths, weaknesses, opportunities and threats.

2 A company's objectives must be clear, quantifiable, timetabled and realistic.

3 Market penetration involves increasing sales of existing products within existing markets.

4 Market development involves selling existing products in new markets.

5 Product development involves producing new products for sale into existing markets.

6 Diversification involves producing new products for new markets.

# Index

# *Essential Elements*

covering the core of modular courses

Further titles in this series...

*Essential Elements of*
## Management Accounting *Jill & Roger Hussey*

**Contents:** The role of management accounting; Cost classification and control; Total costing; Marginal costing; Capital investment and appraisal; Budgetary control; Standard costing; Appendices.

**ISBN** 1 85805 103 7

*Essential Elements of*
## Financial Accounting *Jill & Roger Hussey*

**Contents:** The accounting framework; Users and uses of financial information; The cash flow forecast; The profit and loss account for a sole trader; The balance sheet for a sole trader; The financial statements of a limited company; Interpretation of financial statements.

**ISBN** 1 85805 091 X

*Essential Elements of*
## Business Economics *Mark Sutcliffe*

**Contents:** The UK economy – an overview; Resource allocation; Business costs; The structure of business and its conduct; Small firms and multinationals; Wages and the labour market; Investment, R & D and training; National economic change and business activity; Money, banking and inflation; Economic policy and the business environment; The international dimension; Europe and business.

**ISBN** 1 85805 095 2

*Essential Elements of*
## Human Resource Management *Sally Howe*

**Contents:** An introduction to human resource management; The organisational context; Human resource planning and administration; Employee resourcing; Equalising employment opportunities; Employee development; Reward management; Employee relations.

ISBN 1 85805 145 2

# *Essential Elements*

covering the core of modular courses

Further titles in this series...

*Essential Elements of*
## Business Information Systems *Brian Corr*

**Contents:** Information; Systems Theory; Management; Decision making; Developing information systems; Databases and DBMS, Modelling.

**ISBN** 1 85805 136 3

*Essential Elements of*
## Business Statistics *Les Oakshott*

**Contents:** Survey Methods, Presentation of data, Summarising data, Probability and decision making, The Normal Distribution, Analysis and interpretation of sample data, Testing a hypothesis, Correlation and regression.

**ISBN** 1 85805 104 5

*Essential Elements of*
## Quantitative Methods *Les Oakshott*

**Contents:** Index numbers, Investment appraisal, Time series analysis, Linear programming, Critical path analysis, Stock control methods, Simulation.

**ISBN** 1 85805 098 7

# Tackling Coursework

*Projects, Assignments, Reports and Presentations*

David Parker

This book provides the student with practical guidance on how to approach the coursework requirement of a typical business studies course, i.e. projects, assignments, reports and presentations. The text makes clear the different approaches needed for the different types of coursework, with examples of each in an Appendix, and there is advice on how to conduct research, collect information and present results, in either written or verbal form. It is expected to be used on the following courses: any business studies course at undergraduate (e.g. BABS) or postgraduate (e.g. MBA) level. It would also be useful as a preparatory text for a research degree.

**Contents:**

*Introduction, Dissertations and projects, Essays and papers, Management reports, Seminars and presentations, Research methods.* **Appendices:** *Further reading, Example of a dissertation proposal, Example of citations, Dissertation contents, Example of an essay.*

**1st edition • 96 pp • 215 x 135 mm • 1994 • ISBN 1 85805 101 0**